Rachel
CARSON

Rachel CARSON

VOICE for the EARTH

GINGER WADSWORTH

LERNER PUBLICATIONS COMPANY • MINNEAPOLIS

The sources for the quotations in this book can be found
on pages 119-122.

LIBRARY OF CONGRESS CATALOGING-IN-PUBLICATION DATA

Wadsworth, Ginger.
  Rachel Carson, voice for the earth / by Ginger Wadsworth.
      p.   cm.
  Includes bibliographical references and index.
  Summary: Describes the life and work of the biologist and writer
who helped initiate the environmental movement.
  ISBN 0-8225-4907-7
  1. Carson, Rachel, 1907-1964—Juvenile literature. 2. Ecologists—
United States—Biography—Juvenile literature. 3. Women
conservationists—United States—Biography—Juvenile literature.
[1. Carson, Rachel, 1907-1964. 2. Conservationists.
3. Biologists.] I. Title
QH31.C33W34   1992
574'.092—dc20
[B]
[92]   90-22743
                                                     CIP
                                                      AC

Manufactured in the United States of America

  2   3   4   5   6   97   96   95   94   93   92

Note to the Reader

I am grateful for the help I received from a number of people and organizations. My research began at the Beinecke Library, Yale University in New Haven, Connecticut, where librarians Bill Finley and Patricia Willis helped me review the Rachel Carson Literary Collection. In Lincoln, Massachusetts, I interviewed Paul Brooks—Rachel's editor at Houghton Mifflin—and his wife, Susie Brooks. At Woods Hole, I saw where Rachel Carson first saw the sea and began her study of marine biology. Next, Roger Christie, Rachel's adopted son, introduced me to his infant son, Thomas, and showed me Rachel's summer cabin and beach in Southport, Maine.

Also in Maine, I visited the Nature Conservancy office and several conservancy spots, including the Rachel Carson Salt Pond. I walked the trail through the Rachel Carson National Wildlife Refuge.

During a second research trip, I traveled to Rachel's childhood home in Springdale, Pennsylvania, now the Rachel Carson Homestead, and talked to Evelyn Hirtle, past president. In nearby Pittsburgh, I toured the grounds at Chatham College, formerly Pennsylvania College for Women. At the Rachel Carson Council in Washington, D.C., I interviewed Shirley Briggs, Rachel's longtime friend.

I am also indebted to Wendy Wareham, Dorothy Sterling, Dorothy Thompson Seif, the Freeman family, plus the numerous writers and researchers I have met across the country who are dedicated to sharing Rachel Carson's "voice."

G.W.

*To my mother
Dorothea Abbott Evarts
a diviner in harmony with Mother Earth*

Part of the author's proceeds go to the Nature Conservancy
to help the desert tortoise research program.

Contents

Rachel was a solitary child who spent a great deal of time outdoors, often with her dogs Candy and Pat.

ONE

1907-1919

"I can remember no time when I wasn't interested in the out-of-doors and the whole world of nature."

Rachel clipped the article from the newspaper's book-review section. She scanned the first paragraph.

> Rachel Carson has done it again! This quiet and shy woman has produced another best seller about the sea. However, slender and pretty Miss Carson does not look like she would be at home at the edge of the sea.

Rachel glanced outside. The sun was barely up, yet birds bustled in the pines. Waves lapped against the rocky shore. Rachel gathered up her specimen bottles and slipped her binoculars around her neck. She rolled her pants to her knees, then put on her hat. Perhaps no one would recognize her and she could explore the tide pools alone.

The azaleas and dogwoods were in full bloom when Rachel Louise Carson was born on May 27, 1907, in western

Pennsylvania, hundreds of miles from the Atlantic Ocean. For the first 22 years of her life, Rachel lived on a farm near the Allegheny River.

Rachel's parents had met in the early 1890s—drawn together by their common interest in music. Maria McLean, the daughter of a Presbyterian minister, graduated from the Female Seminary in Washington, Pennsylvania. A school-teacher, she met Robert Carson when he had come to town with a church quartet. His quiet manner and dark good looks attracted her.

They married in 1894. As was customary then, Maria gave up teaching to become a full-time homemaker. Their daughter Marian was born in 1897, and their son, Robert, Jr., was born two years later.

At the turn of the century, the Carson family moved into a white clapboard, four-room house on 65 acres (26 hectares) of land. The two-story house, which had no electricity or indoor plumbing, stood near the top of a hill. Nestled below in a curve of the Allegheny River was the small community of Springdale. Apple trees and maples shaded the frame houses, and the sidewalks were made of boards.

Pittsburgh, Pennsylvania, was 15 miles (24 kilometers) away. Coal mines, iron-smelting factories, and steel mills surrounded the city, and railroads crisscrossed the once heavily wooded countryside.

Rachel was born when Marian was 10 and Robert was 8. Maria kept busy raising her growing family. She sold apples and chickens in town and sewed most of her children's clothes. She taught piano for 50¢ a lesson. With her wire-rimmed glasses, plain clothes, and her hair in a bun at her neck, Maria Carson looked stern. In reality, she was reserved and gentle—qualities she passed on to Rachel.

The Springdale farm-house, above, *and Maria Carson with her three children,* left

While Rachel was growing up, her father worked part of the time at a local electric station. He also dabbled in insurance and real estate. Robert, Sr., was a soft-spoken, well-educated man. Occasionally he walked to the train station and rode to Pittsburgh on business. He probably took an extra white shirt to change into midway through the day. At that time, Pittsburgh was called the Smoky City because steel mills and coal-powered factories blasted black soot into the air day and night.

The Carsons did not mingle much with the townspeople in Springdale. They were a close-knit family and enjoyed each other's company. They came to Springdale to buy manufactured goods when they could afford them. Not earning enough to support his family, Mr. Carson stopped at the bank every so often to arrange a loan.

By the time Rachel was born, Robert and Marian were in school. Rachel did not mind being alone most of the time. She loved to explore the fields and woods, and to wade in the streams that trickled into the Allegheny River. Her dog Candy followed her everywhere.

On some afternoons, Rachel sat on the porch and waited for Robert and Marian to walk home. Half a dozen dogs and cats dozed on the steps. It was fun to hear what her big brother and sister had done at school and to know her turn at school was coming, too.

Everyone did chores. Rachel collected eggs in the barn, even finding an egg or two in the buggy. She pumped water into buckets in the springhouse below the farmhouse. She carried the water into the kitchen, a lean-to attached to the back of the house. Rachel might help Marian snap green beans for supper or make biscuits in the coal-burning stove. She listened to Marian chat about school and friends.

Rachel reads to her dog Candy.

Rachel's mother gave piano lessons on the old upright piano in the parlor. Usually another student waited impatiently on the porch, clutching books of classical music and piano exercises.

After school, Robert went hunting with his rifle in the woods. Sometimes he brought home game, such as squirrels and rabbits, for supper. Rachel hated it when her brother shot wildlife. She wished he would be like Mama who would not even kill a spider in the house, but instead would sweep it gently out the back door.

The Carson children ride a horse, led by their mother, through the orchard.

After the piano lessons and before supper, while Marian and Robert did their schoolwork, Rachel and her mother often took walks in the woodlands near the house. Rachel's mother taught her the names of the wildflowers and the animals that lived in the woods. Sometimes, they watched bees go in and out of a hive, or after dark, they slipped outside to find the Big Dipper or the Milky Way.

Rachel discovered bird nests around the farm. She found snakeskins and feathers and colorful, smooth rocks to save. A conch shell sat on the fireplace mantel in the parlor. Rachel liked to hold the shell to her ear and pretend she could hear the ocean.

Rachel loved books. This love, like her interest in nature, came primarily from her mother. The family had a library in the parlor. Maria Carson started reading to her daughter when she was two. Within a few years, Rachel could read simple books on her own.

In the evenings, the family gathered in the kitchen, near the warmth of the stove, to listen to Maria Carson read. Besides Bible stories, she might have read such classics as *The Last of the Mohicans.* Another favorite at that time was *Freckles*, a popular novel about an orphan boy who loved nature. While Maria read, the room was silent except for an occasional snap or crackle in the stove. A kerosene lantern spilled light onto the pages of her book. Maria's beautiful voice made the words come alive. Rachel sat breathless as she was transported to another place and time. She especially loved the sea poems of John Masefield, such as "Sea Fever," which opened with "I must go down to the seas again, to the lonely sea and the sky."

Many nights, the family gathered around the piano to sing. Or they played Parcheesi. Rachel read Beatrix Potter's animal stories. She knew all the animal characters—Peter Rabbit, Tabitha Twitchet the cat, and Pickles the terrier.

On other nights, while her sister cut out a dress pattern, Rachel cut out paper dolls or went to see what her brother was tinkering with in his "room," a curtained-off area in the kitchen where he slept on a cot. Robert had built a radio from a kit, with wires and a crystal. Once in a while, he let his sister wear the headset and listen to a broadcast from nearby Pittsburgh.

When she was six, Rachel started school at Springdale Elementary. To no one's surprise, she was studious. Since her world until then had been her parents and older brother

Marian and Rachel Carson with Don, Pat, and Candy

and sister, soft-spoken Rachel related well with her teachers. But she was shy with her classmates and did not make friends easily.

She missed a lot of school. When Maria Carson heard of an outbreak of diphtheria, whooping cough, or the measles— serious diseases in those times—she kept Rachel home and taught her herself. Because she was so bright, Rachel easily kept up with her classwork.

When Rachel was nearly 10, her sister was married at the house. Afterward, without Marian around, Rachel felt more alone. In her free time, she wrote stories. Before long, she was designing book jackets to go with her stories. She even made books small enough to fit in her hand.

When Rachel was 10, her isolated world of books and nature was disturbed. The United States entered World War I; soldiers left home to fight in Europe. War news dominated the newspapers and peoples' conversations in town. Robert joined the United States Army Air Service. He went into training as a pilot in Texas. Every day, Rachel checked for letters from her brother. The entire family worried about him and the other American soldiers fighting overseas.

Rachel, Robert, Jr. (in his Army Air Service uniform), and Marian

Rachel painted this red catchfly when she was nine years old.

During this time, Rachel was reading a popular children's magazine, *St. Nicholas.* Her favorite part in the magazine was "St. Nicholas League," written by young readers. One day Rachel decided to write a story for the magazine. She stood at the window in her upstairs bedroom and stared at the pear orchard in bloom. What should she write about? Then she remembered Robert's latest letter home about a brave Canadian pilot. Rachel flopped onto her bed and began her story.

> One day, when he [the Canadian pilot] and one of his companions were flying, a German plane suddenly burst upon them from behind a cloud. The two planes began firing. . . . For awhile, neither plane was injured, but soon . . . a part of one wing of the Canadian aviator's plane had been shot away. The plane wavered, and he knew that if something was not done promptly, the plane would fall. He saw there was only one thing to do, and he did it quickly. He crawled out along the wing, inch by inch, until he reached the end. He then hung from the end of the wing, his weight making the plane balance properly.

That same day, Rachel finished and mailed her story to the magazine. Would *St. Nicholas* pick her story? Long after the pears had been harvested, the September 1918 issue of *St. Nicholas* arrived with "A Battle in the Clouds," by Rachel L. Carson, age ten, Silver Badge Winner. The magazine sent her $10 in prize money—a lot of money at that time.

Thrilled with her success and encouraged by her mother, Rachel created new stories. Soon two other stories also won prizes and were printed in *St. Nicholas*. For her English class, she wrote an essay about *St. Nicholas* magazine. The magazine's advertising department bought it for three dollars and a few cents—a penny per word. Rachel liked to say she became a professional writer at the age of 11.

Maria Carson reads to her daughter.

TWO

1919-1929

"My destiny was somehow linked with the sea."

After the war ended in 1919, Robert, Jr., settled in Pittsburgh and found work as an electrician. By then, Rachel was a high school honor student. At that time, Springdale High was only a two-year school. After those two years of high school, many students ended their education. They found jobs in places such as Springdale's glass factory or the West Penn Power Company.

Mrs. Carson wanted more for her brilliant daughter. So for the next two years, Rachel took the streetcar across the Allegheny River to Parnassus High School. She graduated in May 1925, a few days after her 18th birthday. Her yearbook picture showed an attractive girl with a heart-shaped face. She had large blue eyes and brown hair. Beside her picture was a poem written by her classmates:

> Rachel's like the mid-day sun
> Always very bright
> Never stops her studying
> 'Til she gets it right.

For the young women in 1925, graduation marked a major changing point in their lives. Most of them married and started families or entered the work force. Maria Carson was determined that her daughter should go to college, unlike Robert, Jr., or Marian.

That fall, Rachel enrolled in Pennsylvania College for Women—now Chatham College—a small school in Pittsburgh noted for its academic excellence.

The first few weeks of school were quite an adjustment for Rachel after her sheltered farm life. Three hundred girls shared two dormitories on the campus, ate together, raced back and forth to classes, went to "get-acquainted" teas, and tried out for the school sports teams. Every morning, they attended chapel, and on Sundays, went to church.

Still planning to become a writer, Rachel decided to major in English. In her first composition, she wrote that she was Presbyterian, Scotch-Irish in ancestry, and "intensely fond of anything pertaining to [the] outdoors or athletics."

Rachel loved her English assignments, which explored all kinds of subjects. She wrote a funny story about a black expense book that had been given to her by a well-meaning relative. She called her book a "parasite" because she had to carry it everywhere in case she spent some money. In her story, she planned to toss the little black book into the wastebasket—"never to return!"

She also wrote for her college newspaper—the *Arrow*—and for Omega, a literary club. One of her newspaper stories was about a cat's right to be "independent and as good as anyone else." Like the cat in her story, Rachel was warm and friendly, but a definite individualist.

If she was interested in an activity, she participated with great enthusiasm. She tried out for the freshman basketball team, even though she was only 5'4'' (163 cm). During the winter, she went ice-skating or sledded with her friends on the hill behind the dorm. But when the college held teas, parties, and dances, Rachel seldom participated unless they were an organized part of the school program. She disliked small talk and preferred to study instead.

On many weekends, Maria Carson came to Pittsburgh by train. She stayed the weekend, bringing handmade clothes and a basket of cookies. Sometimes she even typed Rachel's school papers.

As a sophomore, Rachel was required to take a science course. She chose biology. To her surprise, the demanding class reawakened her love of nature. She enjoyed her inspiring young teacher, Mary Skinker, and they became friends.

Two of her classmates, Dorothy Thompson—another scholarship student—and Mary Frye, were also science-oriented. Rachel was happy to make close friends, with similar interests, at college. Led by Mary Skinker, they went on field trips or sat around talking about literature and music—as well as science.

Rachel thought about changing her major to science. She liked science and writing equally. It did not occur to her—or her teachers—to combine the two interests. She sought advice from Miss Skinker and several other professors. Some told her that she had a promising career in writing. Science, they said, was a man's world.

Strongly influenced by the role models of her mother and Mary Skinker, Rachel made her decision in her junior year. She wrote to Mary Frye, who was in Florida. "I have something very exciting to tell you. Get a big breath, Mary! Here goes; I've changed my major. To what? Biology, of

Rachel took classes at Dillworth Hall at Pennsylvania College for Women.

course. Miss Skinker hasn't recovered from the shock yet. She says after this nothing will ever surprise her."

Rachel, who was normally calm and matter-of-fact, enjoyed the sensation her change of major caused on campus. She wrote to Mary later: "You ought to see the reactions I get. I've gotten bawled out and called all sorts of blankety-blank names so much that it's beginning to get monotonous."

To catch up in her new major, Rachel had to take extra classes and spend long hours in the school's cramped, drafty science lab. She peered at slides under her microscope and kept detailed notes about her observations. As a junior and senior, she took heavy class loads that included chemistry, embryology, genetics, bacteriology, and histology—the study of tissues. Her worst subject was math. So her roommate Helen, who was good in math, helped Rachel.

In between studies, Rachel played basketball and tried out for field hockey. She went to the junior prom. She also played pranks on her classmates. When Rachel noticed the

Students walk between classes at Pennsylvania College for Women about the time Rachel Carson was there.

alcohol in the science lab disappearing much too quickly, she added red food coloring and drew a skull and crossbones, the sign of death, on the bottle. From then on, the alcohol supply was not a problem.

Between her junior and senior years, Rachel tutored students at home. Marian and her two small daughters stayed at the house, too. Rachel helped care for her two nieces when Marian was in the hospital, possibly with problems related to diabetes. In a letter to Dorothy, Rachel said she did not have time for creative writing because she was "the chief cook and bottle washer." The house was crowded; guests used a bed in the living room.

Money remained tight in the Carson family. Sometimes the hay and milk bills did not get paid on time. To help pay for some of Rachel's college expenses, Mrs. Carson sold the good china.

By Rachel's senior year, Mary Skinker was working on her Ph.D. at Johns Hopkins University in Maryland. Rachel wrote to her often. She also wrote to Mary Frye that she hoped to get her master's degree in science.

As graduation day approached, Rachel thought more and more about her future. One night in her college dorm, with the rain and wind beating against her window, she read a line from "Locksley Hall" by Alfred, Lord Tennyson: "For the mighty wind arises, roaring seaward, and I go." Rachel later said, "I can . . . remember my intense emotional response as that line spoke to . . . me . . . to tell me that my own path led to the sea—which then I had never seen—and that my own destiny was somehow linked with the sea."

In May of 1929, Rachel graduated with high honors—magna cum laude. That summer, her dream about the sea came true. Thanks to the efforts of Mary Skinker, she received a summer fellowship to study science at Woods Hole Marine Biological Laboratory in Massachusetts and a $200 scholarship to do graduate work the following year at Johns Hopkins University in Baltimore, Maryland.

Rachel was the talk of her classmates and family. At the time, few women graduated from college. Even fewer were awarded a scholarship to earn a higher degree. Rachel, who had just turned 22, took it all in stride.

She packed her bags and journeyed to Washington, D.C., where she visited Mary Skinker, then traveled to New York City by train. Finally, she boarded a small boat to reach Woods Hole, which sat on the heel of Cape Cod.

At Woods Hole, Rachel stepped ashore and looked around. Research ships bobbed at their moorings. The village's brick buildings seemed inviting. First, she registered at the Marine Biological Laboratory, where she would be working. Next, she found the library and the central dining hall where everyone ate. She and Mary Frye, her college friend, who also had won a scholarship, settled into a rented room in a private house.

Rachel wrote to Dorothy that "[Our] room . . . is very comfortably furnished, even to hot and cold running water. My table is in the lab just across the street. There are about four others working in the same room. One's mail is delivered to his laboratory table!"

Rachel and Mary ate with other students and with famous scientists they had known only from their college textbooks. Rachel wondered if someday, after earning her master's degree, she would work with one of the scientists in the room. She noted that few were women.

The six-week-long fellowship sped by quickly. Rachel loved everything about Woods Hole. She studied the sea creatures who lived on the beaches, in the nearby tide pools, and in aquariums filled with seawater. She took her research seriously and worked on a project to study the cranial, or skull, nerves of turtles. Her adviser thought her results might be worth publishing in a scientific journal.

After work, there was time to explore the coast and attend beach parties. Rachel tried to become a better swimmer and get tan, but instead, grew "a crop of freckles."

The summer was another turning point in Rachel's life. She decided to pursue a career in an ocean-related field. She looked forward to her graduate classes at Johns Hopkins University that autumn, where she would focus on marine zoology, the study of sea animals.

One night the mackerel came upon an abando[ned] gill net swaying in the water. The net was buoy[ed] t the surface by cork floats; and from the s[urface] line it hung down [crossed out] — It [was] like a [l]awn tennis net. Its meshes were 2 inches across so that the yearling mackerel could have slipped through, although larger ones would have been gilled in the twine. Tonight no fish would have tried to pass through the net, for all its meshes were hung with tiny warning lamps. [crossed out] Peridinium and Ceratium and — ; Noctiluca — clung [crossed out] the wet twine in the dark sea — the [crossed out] It was as though all the myriad lesser fry of the sea, the animals small as a dust mote, the plants tinier than a — drifting [crossed out] in ocean, [crossed out] seized upon the meshes of the gill net as the one firm — in their fluid world, and clung to it with protoplasmic hair and cilia, with tentacle and — The gill net glowed like a thing alive; its radiance shone out into the black black sea, shone down into the darkness below, and [crossed out] up amphipods and — , — drawn by the light, and these larger creatures also clung to the meshes. As the net gave — to

On a page from the manuscript for Under the Sea-Wind, *Rachel sketched one of her cats.*

THREE

1929-1940

*"A writer's occupation is one of the loneliest in the world. . . .
And so I believe only the person who knows and is not afraid of
loneliness should aspire to be a writer."*

Before graduate school started, Rachel went to the United States Bureau of Fisheries in Washington, D.C. She wanted advice about future jobs. One of the bureau's supervisors, Elmer Higgins, told her that the Bureau of Fisheries had never hired a female scientist. He suggested that she teach science in high school or college.

In a firm voice, Rachel told Elmer Higgins she wanted to become a scientist, not a teacher. Impressed by her quiet manner and her determination to become a scientist, Mr. Higgins asked Miss Carson to stop by after she finished her schooling.

During the first days of classes at Johns Hopkins University, Rachel told herself to complete her education, then worry about her future. Once again, as at Woods Hole, Rachel noticed that most of her teachers and classmates were men. Her classes and laboratory time soon added up to over 40 hours a week. Every night, she had reading and other homework as well.

Rachel had been in graduate school only a few weeks when the stock market crashed in October 1929. People lost jobs and worried about whether they would have enough money to pay their bills. Banks ran out of money. Thousands of factories and businesses shut down. The Great Depression had begun and most Americans' lives changed.

In the early months of 1930, Rachel persuaded her parents to join her in Baltimore and to share a rented house. Robert, Jr., lived with them for a while. Robert, Sr., looked for odd jobs in town and Maria cared for the house. The Carsons, who were in their sixties, worked hard to keep their daughter in school. Despite the depression, the family was happy to have food and a roof over their heads—more than some families who slept in their cars and lined up for free food at welfare agencies or churches.

Besides being a student, Rachel worked part-time as a biology laboratory assistant at Johns Hopkins University and taught zoology during the summers. During the winters, she was a half-time teaching assistant at the University of Maryland since her family was dependent on her income.

One Thanksgiving, Dorothy Thompson, who was getting her master's at Bryn Mawr College in Pennsylvania, came to visit Rachel for the holiday. The little house was full. Marian was there with her five- and seven-year-old daughters, Marjorie and Virginia. Rachel read stories to the two girls in front of the roaring fireplace, one of several that heated the house. After the stories, the girls played with their dolls while Rachel and Dorothy talked about school and work. Robert Carson, Sr., frail and elderly, sat quietly in his chair near the fireplace.

That evening, as everyone climbed into bed, Mrs. Carson came to each room carrying a candle for light. She said good-night to Rachel, then gave Dorothy a hug and a kiss. "That's because you haven't been away from home at a holiday before . . . and you must miss your own mother very much."

After Dorothy took the bus back to college, Rachel went back to long months of work and study. For the next few years, they wrote to one another about their schoolwork. In one letter, Rachel told Dorothy that she had just put in a tough day at the lab. She did everything herself. A lot of glassware needed washing, and she had to see to it that each table was supplied with a long list of apparatus. Sometimes, her specimens died and she had to start her projects over again. Rachel dreamed of studying full-time to become a marine zoologist, but the family still needed her income.

Later, she wrote to Dorothy about one of her hardest classes, biochemistry. At the end of the semester, when the professor handed out the grades, Rachel received an 85 out of 100. For Rachel, that was a low grade, but as she told Dorothy, she was happy just to pass the course.

She started her master's thesis—a major research paper—on the developmental stages of catfish. Rachel conferred with her professors and spent endless hours in the laboratory dissecting catfish and examining parts under her microscope. Three years later, Rachel completed all of her classwork as well as her thesis on the catfish. Johns Hopkins University granted Rachel a master's degree in 1932.

Maria and Robert Carson were proud of their brilliant daughter, but there was little else to celebrate. Times continued to be rough for the family and the rest of the country. Glad to have a job, Rachel continued to teach.

One of Rachel's cats, with a friend, lies under the tree on Christmas morning.

On rainy days or in the evenings, Rachel turned to writing again—poetry this time. Her writing companion was a kitten her brother brought home. Rachel dreamed of seeing her poems in print and earning some money, so she persistently submitted them to most of the major magazines, such as the *Saturday Evening Post, Poetry,* and *Woman's Home Companion.*

In 1935, everything suddenly changed when Robert Carson, Sr., died. Even as she grieved for her father, Rachel knew that her half-time teaching job would not bring in enough income. Her brother had his own life. Her sister, still battling chronic illness, was struggling too.

Practical as always, Rachel stored her unpublished poetry and rejection slips in a desk drawer and went job hunting. Remembering Elmer Higgins's invitation, she visited him at the United States Bureau of Fisheries and told him she needed work.

Mr. Higgins asked Miss Carson if she could write. The bureau was presenting a series of seven-minute radio programs on marine life called "Romance under the Waters." Mr. Higgins was frustrated because none of his assistants could turn scientific language into easy-to-understand programs for regular radio listeners.

Rachel said yes, and Mr. Higgins hired her on the spot, saying, "I've never seen a written word of yours, but I'm going to take a sporting chance." Rachel later commented, "That little job which led to a permanent appointment as a biologist, was in its way, a turning point."

Earning about $19.25 a week at her part-time job, she produced radio broadcasts from Elmer Higgins's office on the first floor of the Commerce Building in Washington, D.C. The only windows faced a courtyard. Outdoor-loving Rachel grumbled that "It [was] like working in the bottom of a well," but she knew she was lucky to have landed a job.

The following year, Rachel's sister Marian died at the age of 40, orphaning her two elementary-school-aged daughters. Rachel and her mother decided to raise Marjorie and Virginia. Rachel was more like a big sister than an aunt. While the girls attended school, Rachel was the breadwinner and Maria took care of the house.

Learning that the United States Bureau of Fisheries needed a junior aquatic biologist, Rachel took the required civil service exam. She was the only woman competing for the job and she got the top score of 97 percent. She became a full-time government employee in 1936, earning $38.48 a week.

Along with her successful, lively radio scripts, Rachel wrote a series of feature articles related to fishing for the *Baltimore Sunday Sun*. The pay was not much—$10 to $20 per article—but Rachel needed the extra money.

After the broadcasts ended, Rachel prepared a series of pamphlets on sea creatures for the Bureau of Fisheries. Mr. Higgins wanted the pamphlets put into a booklet for the staff and asked Rachel to write an accompanying introduction to explain the mysteries of the sea.

Late into the night, Rachel wrote her first draft. Word by word, the long essay changed and took shape. Finally, she finished her introduction, which was about 25 typed pages.

The morning after she finished, Rachel handed a draft to her boss. Seated at his desk, Elmer Higgins read slowly. He finally looked up and, with a twinkle in his eyes, told Miss Carson he could not use it. He explained that her essay was too literary to be in a government booklet and suggested she send her article to the *Atlantic Monthly*.

Rachel took his advice. "Undersea" appeared in the *Atlantic Monthly* in September 1937, and Rachel received $75 for the article. Rachel was ecstatic about her appearance in a national magazine.

Readers loved her article and wrote that they had always wondered what went on beneath the surface of the ocean. They agreed that Rachel's opening lines captured that curiosity:

> Who has known the ocean? Neither you nor I, with our earth-bound senses. . . .
> To sense this world of waters known to the creatures of the sea we must shed our human perceptions of length and breadth and time and place, and enter vicariously into a universe of all-pervading water.

Two of her readers, Quincy Howe, an editor at Simon & Schuster, and Hendrik Willem van Loon, a well-known author, wrote to suggest that Miss Carson do a book on marine life based on "Undersea." With their encouragement, Rachel began her first book.

Rachel wanted *Under the Sea-Wind* to flow like a novel. To make her subject come alive, she used a main character — the sea. Rachel outlined three sections: one about life at the shore, one in the open sea, and another on the bottom of the sea. Her supporting cast included shorebirds, mackerels, and

Rachel gave her readers a sense of "all-pervading water" in Under the Sea-Wind.

Rachel wrote about shorebirds at dusk in the chapter entitled "Flood Tide."

eels. She gave her characters some human characteristics, such as fear and a sense of time, so that readers could more easily understand the full flavor of marine life.

Every evening after work, Rachel escaped upstairs to a large bedroom to write in peace and quiet. Two Persian cats, Buzzie and Kito, joined her. Buzzie slept on the writing table, sprawled across a pile of notes and manuscript pages next to the typewriter.

She averaged two pages a night; on a good day she produced six pages. The writing was painfully slow. Rachel liked doing the research more than the work of turning out a manuscript.

Rachel wrote her first drafts in longhand and then switched to her typewriter. Once, twice, 10 times if necessary, she rewrote and revised until she was pleased with her words. She believed that "writing is largely a matter of . . . hard work, of writing and rewriting endlessly until you are satisfied that you have said what you want to say. . . . For me, that usually means many, many revisions."

From time to time, her mother read the text aloud to her. If the words sounded like "a confused tangle of phrases," Rachel rolled a fresh sheet of paper into her typewriter and started over.

When she had a difficult time falling asleep after writing half the night, she turned to a stack of books on her bedside table for relaxation. Nature essays and poetry appealed to her, and she loved sea books like *Moby Dick*. One of her favorite authors was Englishman Harry Williamson, who wrote *Tarka the Otter* and *Salar the Salmon*. Rachel wrote, "He has influenced my writing more than anyone else."

As Rachel wrote and rewrote and polished her book at night and worked for the government during the day, she followed the beginning of the war in Europe. Rachel still remembered World War I: war-related newspaper headlines, legless veterans on the streets of Pittsburgh, and neat new rows of crosses in the cemeteries. Would the young men she knew have to put on uniforms? Would her married friends— many with small children—have to send their spouses overseas?

Most everyone was preoccupied with the war. Only a few friends and Rachel's mother, who typed the final manuscript, knew about the book. On the last day of 1940, Rachel delivered *Under the Sea-Wind* to Simon & Schuster in New York. She could not wait to see her first book in print.

FOUR

1941–1945

"I decided to write a book that would summarize what modern man knows of the sea."

Eleven months later, a cardboard box arrived. Rachel quickly opened the flaps; inside lay her copies of her book. Rachel picked up the book gingerly, feeling the glossy jacket and smelling the fresh ink. She skimmed her introduction, in which she explained that *Under the Sea-Wind*

> was written to make the sea and its life as vivid a reality for those who may read the book as it has become for me during the past decade. . . .
>
> To stand at the edge of the sea, to sense the ebb and the flow of the tides, to feel the breath of a mist moving over a great salt marsh, to watch the flight of the shore birds that have swept up and down the surf lines of the continents for untold thousands of years, to see the running of the old eels and the young shad to the sea, is to have knowledge of things that are as nearly eternal as any earthly life can be. These things were before ever man stood on the shore of the ocean and looked out upon it with wonder; they continue year in, year out, through the centuries and the ages, while man's kingdoms rise and fall.

Rachel dedicated the book to her mother. At work she handed a copy to her boss. Inside, Rachel had inscribed, "To Mr. Higgins who started it all." She sent thank-you notes to everyone who had worked on the book, from her copy editor to her publisher.

On November 1, 1941, *Under the Sea-Wind* appeared on shelves at bookstores across the country. In one of the first reviews, The *New York Herald Tribune* stated that "there is drama in every sentence. She rouses our interest in this ocean world and we want to watch it." Rachel, who was 34, anticipated a long, successful career as a writer.

Five weeks later, on December 7, 1941, Japan bombed Pearl Harbor in Hawaii. President Roosevelt declared war, and *Under the Sea-Wind*, like most everything else, was swiftly forgotten. Once again, Americans immersed themselves in war. Men signed up to fight for their country; women joined the war effort by working in munitions factories. Across the continent, food and gasoline were rationed. Americans read newspapers filled with war news, not books about the sea.

The first year, the book sold only 1,348 copies. Rachel's earnings came to under a thousand dollars, and her dreams of being a successful writer were shattered by events beyond her control. She wrote to a friend: "If one is to live even in part by writing, he may as well look at the facts. Except for the rare miracles where a book becomes a 'best seller,' I am convinced that writing a book is a very poor gamble financially."

Although discouraged by the low sales, Rachel was pleased with the positive reviews and especially with the book's reception among scientists. Dr. William Beebe, undersea explorer and marine biologist, wrote, "Miss Carson's science cannot be questioned." Later, Dr. Beebe would include two of Rachel's chapters in his anthology, *The Book of Naturalists.*

Dr. Beebe wrote to Rachel to praise her book, starting a friendship and a lifelong exchange of serious ideas. Rachel began similar correspondence with several other well-known scientists. One scientist told her that *Under the Sea-Wind* "will be as good ten years from now as it is today." Rachel found that hard to visualize.

It had been a challenge to write the book and keep up with work. Since 1940, all government agencies had been preparing for possible war, and the Bureau of Fisheries was no exception. The bureau merged with the Biological Survey to form the new Fish and Wildlife Service, under the Department of the Interior.

The war effort required that the government know as much as possible about the sea and coastlines to protect United States pilots and sailors from the enemy. Although Rachel was not involved in the actual research, she wanted to read every report—from the latest weather information to maps showing hidden undersea canyons and reefs.

Government reports on chemical use crossed her desk too. In Italy, soldiers were dusted with the pesticide DDT to prevent the outbreak of typhoid. She worried about the effects of these chemicals on human beings and the rest of nature. She thought about her mother's "reverence for life," which had been passed on to her.

After the war, much of this new information—some good and some frightening—would have to be studied. Rachel wanted to be part of it. Maybe she would write another book. In the meantime, she gathered information and recorded her thoughts. She was too busy to do much else.

Early each morning, Rachel hurried to her office. She unlocked the door and flipped on the lights. Her large office contained walls of books and a photograph of a blue crab. Rachel made sure her door was open so her coworkers knew she had arrived.

No longer a junior aquatic biologist, Rachel had been promoted several times. She had more responsibilities, including writing conservation bulletins for the Fish and Wildlife Service. Rachel crammed each booklet with easy-to-read facts. Her job was to popularize seafood as a new, protein-rich source of food, since most available meat was being shipped overseas to the soldiers.

Rachel was one of two women working for the Fish and Wildlife Service in a capacity other than clerical. She did not think of herself as a feminist and commented later in life that "I'm not interested in things done by women or by men but in things done by people."

When Bob Hines, a wildlife artist, joined the staff, he was not sure he wanted a "lady supervisor." He soon learned that Miss Carson "was a very able executive. . . . She knew how to get things done the quickest, simplest . . . [most] direct way. She had the sweetest, quietest 'no' any of us had ever heard. She had *standards*, high ones."

In 1945, Shirley Briggs joined the Fish and Wildlife Service as a graphic artist and writer. Her office was next to Rachel's, and the two women became friends. With Shirley and a handful of other friends, Rachel laughed easily and played pranks when government bureaucracy became boring. In the privacy of her office, Rachel could "blow off steam" to Shirley about incompetent writers.

Wartime Washington, D.C., was full of scientists. Many were bird-watchers, like Shirley and Rachel, who joined the

Rachel's love of nature also drew her to the mountains. Here she perches atop Hawk Mountain, in Pennsylvania, to watch the hawks.

local Audubon Society. On the weekends, Shirley, Rachel, and others scoured the countryside for birds and wildlife. In the fall, they watched the hawk migration in Pennsylvania.

Many of these scientists formed lasting friendships. They gathered at informal parties, where they discussed not only the latest scientific information, but music, art, and writing. Shirley recalled that "Rachel appreciated so many kinds of people, and was always glad to meet new ones and enter into whatever conversation or merriment was going on at these affairs."

For the Carson household, it was a happy time despite the war. Marjorie and Virginia were busy teenagers. Rachel enjoyed hearing about the girls' activities. And they both turned to Rachel for advice on school problems or boyfriends.

On weekends, Maria Carson, who was in her 70s, frequently took care of the house and her granddaughters so Rachel could spend time with her friends. Rachel tried to get to the beach often. Although she dreamed of traveling all over the world, she had to do most of her exploring nearby because of her responsibilities at work and at home.

Rachel did not complain. She enjoyed early morning and nighttime walks. Nature was literally out her back door and waiting to be discovered. Often, she jotted down her discoveries in little notebooks. In one unpublished paper, she wrote:

> Here on my woodpile I have become acquainted with a half dozen spiders, permanent, respectable residents who have spun their funnel webs. . . . One of these spiders I came to know rather well. Every night I visited the woodpile I made a point of peeping down her funnel to see whether she was still there. One night I was startled to see a strange spider—a larger, hairier, more sinister looking creature occupying the funnel. . . . I saw, deep in the funnel, a little body that looked like the remains of a spider. I could only surmise that some dark internecine tragedy had overtaken my friend.

With encouragement from her friends, Rachel decided to try to sell magazine articles. Once again, Rachel wrote late into the night while Buzzie and Kito batted pencils about and dove in and out of the trash can.

Rachel broke into *Reader's Digest* with a story about bats and their use of "radar" to avoid obstacles in the dark. Soon after that, she sold a second story on chimney swifts—small, gray birds that often nest in chimneys.

Despite her busy schedule, Rachel grew restless at work. She applied unsuccessfully for an editorial job at *Reader's Digest*, and she asked the National Audubon Society to consider her if an opening occurred. In a letter to a friend, she wrote, "No, my life isn't at all well ordered and I don't know where I am going! I know that if I could choose what seems to me the ideal existence, it would be just to live by writing."

In 1945, the United States dropped two atomic bombs on Japan. Thousands of Japanese were killed and the war ended. Now, the world had a new, deadly, manufactured weapon. Rachel had been raised to believe that "the stream of life would flow on through time in whatever course God had appointed for it . . . without interference from one of the drops of the stream, man."

Atomic warfare proved Rachel's deepest beliefs to be wrong, and she began to change her philosophy of life. Human beings could interfere with the earth and change it forever. The atomic bomb and those government reports on chemicals confirmed it.

Rachel's writing echoes the rhythm and poetry of the sea.

FIVE

1945-1951

"If there is poetry in my book about the sea, it is not because I deliberately put it there but because no one could write truthfully about the sea and leave out the poetry."

The workday had barely begun, but Rachel's mind whirled with the tasks ahead. Uncovering her typewriter, she thought about the staff meeting at 10:00. Her eyes drifted to a neat stack of manuscripts on her desk. Would she find time to edit them all today or end up taking some home as usual?

After lunch, she met with an illustrator. Together, they reviewed the final layout for a pamphlet. Rachel smiled to herself. Since becoming the chief editor for the Fish and Wildlife Service, it seemed as if she headed a small publishing house.

Rachel ran a tight, efficient office, supported by her loyal staff. If necessary, she politely criticized sloppy work, even work submitted by scientists who outranked her. As Bob Hines, one of her staff members, recalled, she "had no patience with dishonesty or shirking [work] in any form."

During the late 1940s, Rachel decided to have the Fish and Wildlife Service publish 12 illustrated booklets on the national wildlife refuges, land set aside to protect animal and plant species. The booklets would be titled *Conservation in Action* and were intended to teach Americans to conserve natural resources.

Since World War II, industrialization had been changing the face of the United States and the philosophy of its people. With little thought of any future impact, developers were replacing farmlands with houses and towns while cars rolled off the assembly lines to travel on miles of new highways.

Whenever she could, Rachel visited the wildlife refuges with Shirley Briggs or another colleague. Rachel filled her battered suitcase with rugged clothes, a hat to protect her fair skin, a hand lens for checking out specimens up close, camera equipment, and a small spiral notebook to record her observations. She never left home without her binoculars.

A sunrise seen from Assateague Island

In April 1946, Rachel and Shirley traveled to Chincoteague, Virginia, on the southern end of Assateague Island on the Maryland border. For several days, they explored the island, photographed clams and oysters, studied the birds, and climbed to the top of the lighthouse. They also helped rescue two ponies mired in the tidal flats.

Finished with her work at Chincoteague and back in her office, Rachel worked on her booklets before heading to another refuge. The booklets would not be typical government documents, but would clearly evoke the beauty of each refuge. In her introduction, Rachel pleaded for human beings to coexist peacefully with nature:

> Wild creatures, like men, must have a place to live. As civilization creates cities, builds highways, and drains marshes it takes away, little by little, the land that is suitable for wildlife. And as their spaces for living dwindle, the wildlife populations themselves decline.

In 1948, while working full-time for the government, Rachel started another book about the sea. In some ways, she had been working on this book since childhood, when she first became intrigued with the sea and its life. She wanted *The Sea Around Us* to be a book that she had searched for on the library shelves but never found, one that would be easy to understand and imaginatively appealing to readers untrained in science.

For her book, Rachel continued to review the latest government information on the sea. Friends and coworkers, among them Bob Hines, helped her stack library books on the back seat of her car. At home, she studied them and took notes. She corresponded with oceanographers throughout the world.

Rachel also asked private and special collections libraries to search for obscure information. She consulted over 1,000 separate printed sources. After the spring thaw, Rachel headed for the Atlantic Coast. One of her favorite spots for gathering information was along the coast near Boothbay, Maine.

After completing a few chapters, Rachel decided to hire a literary agent to help her find a publisher. Rachel chose Marie Rodell, a former writer and book editor. They began what would be a lifelong friendship and partnership.

Marie submitted the first third of the book and an outline to Oxford University Press. In June of 1949, Rachel signed a contract with them. On hearing the news, Dr. Beebe told Rachel that she could not write the book until she put her head under water.

Rachel laughed at Dr. Beebe's comment. She admitted that "I am a disappointment to my friends who expect me to be completely nautical. I swim indifferently. . . am only mildly enthusiastic about seafoods, and do not keep tropical fish as pets." But she took Dr. Beebe's advice.

The following month, accompanied by Shirley, Rachel took what she called "The Great Undersea Adventure" off the Florida coast. She donned a metal diving helmet, added lead weights to her feet, and went down 15 feet (5 meters) to get a firsthand look at the undersea world she knew so well. She disliked the sound of the air coming into the helmet, but at least she'd been "swimming" with the colorful creatures of the coral reef.

Then Rachel decided to take a 10-day sea voyage to the famous fishing grounds, Georges Bank, 200 miles (322 kilometers) east of Boston, Massachusetts. The *Albatross III*, a fishing trawler converted to a research vessel, operated out of Woods Hole. Rachel asked to sign on.

Rachel waits, with her metal helmet at her feet, to go diving in "The Great Undersea Adventure."

Right away, she ran into an obstacle: no woman had ever been on the *Albatross III*. In fact, women were seldom allowed on ships then. Sailors believed that women on board brought bad luck. But Rachel was determined. For her book, she wanted to learn about deep-sea fish populations. Rachel made a deal with the captain. She would bring along her agent, Marie Rodell, so that she would not be alone with 50 men.

The two women boarded the 179-foot (55-meter)-long ship, which looked small and uninviting. Marie clutched her bottle of Dramamine—a medicine for motion sickness. The crew warned Rachel and Marie to always be hanging onto

The Albatross III *was a research vessel for the Fish and Wildlife Service. It was used to learn the facts necessary to maintain the fisheries in the northwest Atlantic.*

something because the *Albatross III* "rolled like a canoe in a sea [and] everyone got violently seasick." Another crew member leered and said, "Never a trip without an accident."

The first night, as they lay in their bunks, the two women heard bangs, clangs, and rumbles overhead. They jerked upright. What was happening? Suddenly, Rachel realized that a trawler fishes . . . day and night. Huge squeaking winches were hauling up nets full of fish. Rachel and Marie could expect to hear the banging every night, but they did not dare complain of the noise. The next morning, the women smiled brightly and told the men that they thought they had heard a mouse once, but they were too sleepy to care.

Rachel survived the friendly teasing from the crew and, at the same time, gained valuable information for her book. Several times, she slipped a hydrophone over her ears and listened to underwater sounds. She watched a depth recorder trace the ups and downs of the ocean floor. On foggy days, she examined fish and studied plankton under a microscope in the ship's laboratory.

Back home again, Rachel worried about money. Aware of her financial problems, Dr. Beebe recommended her for the Eugene F. Saxton Memorial Fellowship, an award providing financial assistance to writers. Rachel received $2,250, making it possible for her to take a few months off from work. During late 1949 and part of 1950, Rachel was able to write whenever she wanted. Even so, the pressure got to her and she wrote, "I feel now that I'd die if this went on much longer." Sometimes she was too tired to sleep.

When the money ran out, she returned to work. Once again, Rachel wrote at night. Sometimes, she went from her typewriter at home to her typewriter at work without sleeping. Rachel said that "the work was just plain hard slogging . . . searching in the . . . technical papers of scientists for the kernels of fact to weld into my profile of the sea." She complained to Marie that "not a single morning bird walk, and spring almost gone. I . . . don't seem to have the energy to tuck that in, too."

In that spring of 1950, Rachel learned that her friend and first college science teacher, Mary Skinker, was very ill. She borrowed some money and flew to her bedside in Chicago for one last visit.

After the trip, Rachel finished her book. Eighty-one-year-old Maria Carson typed the final draft. Marie Rodell submitted chapters of *The Sea Around Us* to several popular magazines for the possible sale of individual chapters to a magazine.

Before the book came out, one chapter appeared in *Yale Review*, another in *Science Digest*. Finally, the *New Yorker* published half the book in three parts. The *New Yorker*'s payment nearly equaled a full year's salary at Rachel's government job.

She had little time to celebrate, however, because she had so many decisions to make about the book. Being a perfectionist, Rachel agonized over the title. Was it right? How should the chapters be arranged? Before the book went to press, Rachel scrutinized every word . . . every comma. She did not want to find a single mistake later.

A few weeks before the book came out, Rachel sensed that *The Sea Around Us* would change her life. Already, stacks of fan mail were pouring in from the *New Yorker* serialization. Then she won the $1,000 George Westinghouse Award from the American Association for the Advancement of Science for the best science writing to appear in a magazine in 1950.

A warm, Carolina beach

Before *The Sea Around Us* was launched by Oxford University Press with a party, Rachel escaped to a beach in North Carolina. For two weeks she climbed over rocks and waded out to shoals, enjoying the ocean alone. She wrote to Marie that "my legs got absolutely cooked . . . my face and arms have fared better, but are considerably weathered-looking. So I'm thanking my stars I didn't buy a pink dress for the party."

The Sea Around Us was released on July 2, 1951. From that day on, the main challenge was to keep the book in stock.

Bob Hines and Rachel search for specimens in a Florida tide pool.

SIX

1952-1953

*"There is one quality that characterizes all of us who
deal with the sciences of the earth and its life—we are never
bored. We can't be. Every mystery solved brings us to the
threshold of a greater one."*

Unable to keep up with demands for the book, Oxford
University Press made duplicate printing plates so two printers
could work simultaneously. Within a few weeks, *The Sea
Around Us* spiraled up the *New York Times* best-seller list
where it remained for 86 weeks, 39 of them in first place.
The Sea Around Us was published in England and eventually
appeared in more than 30 languages.

Now 44, Rachel was well on her way to becoming an
international celebrity. Maria enjoyed her daughter's new
status. She clipped reviews and helped with business correspondence. The phone rang constantly at the Carson household as relatives and friends called to share in the good news.

The *New York Times* called *The Sea Around Us*

> a publishing phenomenon rare as a total solar eclipse.
> Great poets from Homer . . . down to Masefield have
> tried to evoke the deep mystery and endless fascination

of the ocean, but the slender, gentle [Miss Carson] seems to have the best of it. Once or twice in a generation does the world get a physical scientist with literary genius. . . . Miss Carson has written a classic.

Similar reviews poured in; all were favorable. Bookstores decorated their front windows with pictures of the sea and stacks of her books.

Anxious fans wanted to know all about her. One wrote, "Please let me know in a hurry who Rachel Carson is. That girl keeps me awake night after night." Because Rachel's picture was not on the book jacket, some readers speculated about her age and gender. One man wrote, "I assume from

Rachel sits on a dock at Woods Hole writing publicity for The Sea Around Us.

the author's knowledge that he must be a man." Another writer guessed that Rachel was gray-haired and wise because she knew so much. Another wanted a wife but figured Rachel was too old for him because the book must have taken a long time to write.

Despite all the excitement over *The Sea Around Us*, Rachel's mind whirled with new book projects. Whenever she could, she jotted down notes. Before *The Sea Around Us* was finished, she had started a new book—a guide to the Atlantic seashore for amateur naturalists.

As always, money problems loomed. Rachel had applied for a Guggenheim Fellowship in October of 1950, hoping to receive a financial grant so she could continue to write her new book.

Filling in the lengthy application, Rachel wrote that she needed to do "refresher work" at such places along the Atlantic Coast as the Marine Biological Laboratory at Woods Hole, Duke University in North Carolina, and the University of Miami at Coral Gables, Florida, as well as additional fieldwork. She anticipated all this would take six months, including research time at the Library of Congress in Washington, D.C., and other libraries.

The Guggenheim Foundation granted Rachel $4,000 in April of 1951, enabling her to take a leave of absence from the Fish and Wildlife Service.

That summer, just as *The Sea Around Us* reached bookstores across the country and inched up the best-seller list, Rachel and her mother drove to the coast of North Carolina to work on *The Edge of the Sea*. In the back of the car was another "full-fledged associate," a gray kitten named Muffin. He ended up traveling about 2,000 miles (3220 km) with Rachel and her mother as they explored the Atlantic seashore.

In Beaufort, North Carolina, they encountered zealous fans. One morning, a woman knocked on the door of their motel room, pushed past Mrs. Carson, and handed two copies of *The Sea Around Us* to Rachel, demanding she autograph them both. Rachel was still in bed.

At another point on the trip, Rachel was sitting under a hair dryer in a beauty parlor when an admirer asked to meet her. As Rachel recalled, "I admit I felt hardly at my best, with a towel around my neck and my hair in pin curls." She later told Marie and her publishers, enough is enough! "I'm pleased to have people say nice things about the book, but all this stuff about me seems odd, to say the least."

Rachel escaped to the beach. She donned her swimming suit and sneakers and waded into tide pools. There, she

Rachel searches through a tide pool near her cottage in Maine.

studied sea creatures and peered into her water telescope, which looked like a bucket with a glass bottom. From time to time, Rachel put on her face mask and floated quietly, breathing through her snorkel. She joined her mother on the beach, spotting birds through her binoculars.

Jellyfish and seaweed in a Maine tide pool

When Rachel returned home, her mailbox was filled with fan letters and requests for speaking engagements. Marie's desk overflowed with the same kind of mail. At first, Rachel turned down all invitations. She was not good at small talk with strangers or at public speaking.

That fall, an editor from the *New York Herald Tribune* convinced her to speak at a "book-and-author luncheon" in New York City. Weeks before the speech, Rachel wrote out her text. She polished her draft, practicing in front of her mother and the cat. When the moment arrived, Rachel almost bolted when she found herself facing an audience of 1,500. In a low voice, she carefully read her prepared text, which included a recording of clicking shrimps and other undersea noises. The speech was a success, and from then on, Rachel spoke to various organizations but stuck to her preplanned words.

The year 1952 started out with a bang. In January, Rachel accepted the Henry G. Bryant Medal from the Geographical Society of Philadelphia—the first ever conferred on a woman—for distinguished service in geography. *The Sea Around Us* received the John Burroughs Medal for outstanding literary quality in the field of natural history. At the end of the month, Rachel accepted the National Book Award for the best nonfiction book of 1951.

In her acceptance speech for the National Book Award, Rachel described her amazement at the popularity of the book, especially since humans played so small a role. She spoke of the letters she received "from all sorts of people, from college presidents to fishermen and from scientists to housewives. Most of these people say that it [the book's popularity] is because the book has taken them away from the stress and strain of human problems. . . and that they have welcomed it."

Referring to humanity's relative insignificance among all life, she concluded by saying, "such letters make me wonder if we have not too long been looking through the wrong end of the telescope. . . . Perhaps if we reversed the telescope and looked at man down these long vistas, we should find less time and inclination to plan for our own destruction."

That year, the nation's newspapers nominated Rachel "Woman of the Year in Literature." A movie studio in Hollywood negotiated with Marie Rodell to do a feature-length documentary film of *The Sea Around Us*. Later, Rachel said she disliked the film because the Hollywood scriptwriters made so many scientific errors. Even so, the film won an Oscar for the year's best full-length documentary.

In the spring of 1952, Rachel accepted three honorary degrees, including Doctor of Literature from Chatham College. Following the ceremony, the alumnae honored Rachel with a tea. While shaking her classmates' hands, Rachel's mind drifted miles away. When a friend asked if she felt all right, Rachel smiled and said she was much more at home barefoot in the sand or on board a ship in sneakers than on hardwood floors in high heels.

While Rachel experienced the life of a famous author, her agent worked busily behind the scenes. Marie decided to press for republication of *Under the Sea-Wind*, Rachel's first book, published in 1941. Oxford University Press bought the rights to republish the book from Simon & Schuster, the original publisher. They issued a new edition of the book in April 1952. *Life* magazine printed part of it, and *Under the Sea-Wind* became an alternate selection for the Book-of-the-Month Club in June.

Rachel was delighted to see *Under the Sea-Wind* back in print. She knew that without the success of *The Sea Around*

Us, her first—and favorite—book might never have been read again. Almost 40,000 copies of *Under the Sea-Wind* were sold before publication. For a while, both books appeared on the nonfiction best-seller list. Delighted critics raved about Rachel's firsthand, warm knowledge of the ocean and her ability to fuse poetry and science. A Chicago reviewer wrote that *Under the Sea-Wind* "has the clearness and the depth of uncontaminated ocean water."

For the first time, Rachel realized she could live her dream of becoming a full-time, independent writer. By then, the royalties—her percentage of the money from the sale of each book—from *The Sea Around Us* and *Under the Sea-Wind* had given her financial security. She returned her Guggenheim Fellowship, and on June 3, 1952, she officially resigned from the Fish and Wildlife Service.

The next year, Rachel realized another longtime dream. She bought a tract of wooded land in West Southport, Maine, which overlooked Sheepscot Bay, and built a one-story summer cottage on the rocks. Her house perched near the tidemark; the rocky beach curved below. The woods and tide pools would be a constant source of study.

During July, Rachel and her mother moved in. Paneled walls and pine ceilings smelled of the forest. The linoleum sparkled, as did windows framed with print curtains. Simple rattan furniture with soft cushions faced the fireplace and the oceanfront window. Off the living room, in her plain, pine-paneled office, Rachel worked at a built-in desk and bookcase. One window faced the water, another looked into the towering trees.

That first year, Rachel stayed as long as she could, enjoying the fall colors and the migrating birds, eating her breakfast with binoculars in one hand so as not to miss anything.

Rachel's cottage in Maine, above, *and the Maine shoreline,* left

Rachel talks with children she has met on a walk near her home.

SEVEN

1954-1957

*"If I had influence with the good fairy who is supposed to
preside over the christening of all children I should ask that
her gift to each child in the world be a sense of wonder so
indestructible that it would last throughout life."*

After the first spring thaw in 1954, Rachel drove her
mother and Jeffie, the cat, toward Maine and Southport
Island. She could not wait to get to her summer cottage.

That afternoon at the cabin, after settling her mother
down for a nap, Rachel opened every window to fill the
house with sea smells and the scent of sun-baked evergreens.
As she emptied the car, Rachel heard a black-throated green
warbler, then spotted a phoebe nesting under the eaves of
her cabin. She made sure the water was turned on and the
phone connected. Then Rachel carefully unpacked her pow-
erful microscope and set it up on her worktable.

With her chores complete, she grabbed her binoculars
and hurried down the steep, wooden stairway from the house
to the beach. She sat on a rock to watch the light fade from
the sky. Seawater lapped gently against the shore and an
osprey flapped by, a silver fish hooked in its talons.

Tomorrow, thought Rachel, as she retraced her steps to the house, tomorrow I will work on my book. After all, she told herself, "for the first time, I'm writing about something while it is right under my nose."

Later, Rachel phoned her neighbor, Dorothy Freeman, to let her know she and her mother had arrived. Dorothy and

Stanley, Dorothy, and Rachel in Maine

her husband Stanley lived in a summer cottage a half mile inland along Sheepscot Bay. The summer before, when Dorothy had read in the local newspaper that Rachel Carson was building a house nearby, she decided to greet the famous new resident.

Although Rachel seldom made friends easily or quickly, the two women became friends right away. Dorothy had summered on the island all her life and now shared her favorite spots with Rachel. With other nature buffs, they formed a telephone hot line. If Dorothy spotted a whale or a school of porpoises, she alerted Rachel, and vice versa.

That summer, Rachel planned to finish furnishing the cabin and start a wildflower garden. She would go on lots of picnics with the Freemans and her mother. She hoped her nieces would visit frequently. Rachel particularly looked forward to seeing Marjorie's young son, Roger.

A large stack of mail from her readers sat on her desk . . . waiting. Rachel sighed, thinking of the effort required to answer the letters. One came from a college student asking her advice on a career; another came from a 90-year-old lady seeking a quiet beach spot. Rachel needed a schedule. Otherwise, when would she find time to write?

All summer, Rachel did much of her fieldwork during the low tides, the best times for making observations and collecting. Following every storm, she checked out the sand-bars and reefs in case anything new or unusual had washed up.

Rachel had been working on *The Edge of the Sea* off and on for several years. The book had gone through several, often painful, stages. Rachel did not want to simply list all the species like earlier seashore guides she had read. Instead, she wanted to write about ecology—the idea that each plant or animal belongs to a community. Just as her readers lived in communities, so did the creatures of the sea. Her aim was "to take the seashore out of the category of scenery and make it come alive. . . . An ecological concept will dominate the book."

Over and over again, Rachel rewrote the book. In a letter to her editor at Houghton Mifflin, Paul Brooks, she wrote, "I am suffering tortures over the manuscript, but I guess that is a normal sign with me."

Finally, the manuscript took shape. Rachel divided the book to describe three living communities: the rocky shores north of Cape Cod, which are affected by tides; the sand beaches southward from Cape Cod, which are dominated by waves; and the coral reefs and mangrove tree coasts of the far south, which are ruled primarily by ocean currents.

Detail of a Florida coral reef

The rocky coast of Maine, above, *and the waves off the Maryland shore,* right

Rachel works with Bob Hines to find snapping shrimp in a sea sponge.

For this book, she worked with her longtime friend and colleague from the Fish and Wildlife Service, Bob Hines, who would do the illustrations. Since Bob preferred to sketch live animals in their native habitats, he and Rachel worked together on the beaches, rocks, and coral reefs of the Atlantic Coast from Florida to Maine. Rachel's mother often accompanied them, writing letters in the car or sitting on a blanket on the beach.

Bob and Rachel wore old sneakers on the rocks. Rachel walked slowly, careful where she put each foot so as not to step on an animal or slip on the barnacle-covered rocks. At her waist, she wore a biologist's belt loaded with specimen bottles.

In many ways, Bob Hines was like a big brother to Rachel. He worried about her falling on the rocks or catching cold from being in the icy water. Bob often joined Rachel and her family at Southport Island for picnics and work.

That summer, Bob and Rachel gathered buckets of sea creatures and plants from tide pools. Back in her cottage, Rachel studied such things as living fronds of seaweed, tube worms, and tiny snails under her microscope. Beside her, Bob sketched. In small, spiral notebooks, she penciled in

Rachel observes tide pool specimens through her microscope.

detailed paragraphs about the behavior and appearance of each specimen she examined. Artist and scientist worked quickly. Afterward, everything went back in the saltwater-filled bucket. Then Bob and Rachel climbed down the steps and returned each animal and plant to its home in the tide pool.

During the long winter months, Rachel completed the manuscript at her home in Silver Spring. She mailed the text to Houghton Mifflin. Rachel told Paul Brooks to make sure that information about Bob Hines appeared on the jacket. After all, he had contributed 160 illustrations. She dedicated the book to "Dorothy and Stanley Freeman, who have gone down with me into the low-tide world and have felt its beauty and its mystery."

Before *The Edge of the Sea* came out in the fall of 1955, several chapters appeared in the *New Yorker*, and a condensed version was included in *Reader's Digest*. Before long, *The*

One of Bob Hines's illustrations for The Edge of the Sea, *which*

Edge of the Sea made the *New York Times* best-seller list and stayed there for 23 weeks.

Again, Rachel collected rave reviews. The *Christian Science Monitor*'s reviewer wrote, "Miss Carson's pen is as poetic as ever and the knowledge she imparts is profound." She received the Achievement Award of the American Association of University Women and, from the National Council of Women of the United States, a citation for the outstanding book of the year.

For Rachel, 1956 was a wonderful year. She was highly successful in the world of literature and science. But she refused to let fame change her life. She enjoyed seeing and exchanging letters with old friends and family. She drove her same old car.

That summer, with Marjorie's son, Roger, in mind, she wrote a magazine article about sharing nature with children.

includes a sand dollar, a moon snail, and a ghost crab

"Help Your Child to Wonder" appeared in *Women's Home Companion*. Ten years later, it would be published in book form as *The Sense of Wonder*. In the opening paragraph, Rachel wrote:

> One stormy autumn night when my nephew Roger was about 20 months old I wrapped him in a blanket and carried him down to the beach in the rainy darkness. Out there, just at the edge of where-we-couldn't-see, big waves were thundering in, dimly seen white shapes that boomed and shouted and threw great handfuls of froth at us. Together we laughed for pure joy—he a baby meeting for the first time the wild tumult of Oceanus, I with the salt of a half a lifetime of sea love in me. But I think we felt the same spine-tingling response to the vast, roaring ocean and the wild night around us.

"The vast, roaring ocean"

The summer was hectic. At 87, Maria Carson was crippled with arthritis and needed constant care. Marjorie suffered from diabetes. Day after day, Rachel drove both women to the local clinic for treatments. Friends visited constantly, arriving by car and boat. Although Rachel took them for walks in the woods and down to the tide pools, she wrote to Marie Rodell, "I'm weary and think of putting a chain across the road with a sign, 'Rachel Carson will return from the Antarctic in November.'"

Despite her busy schedule, Rachel's mind filled with new dreams. From friends, she sought advice about turning her part of the island into a sanctuary, a protected place where people could explore nature. When she had enough money saved, Rachel hoped to buy part of the coastline. In the meantime, she helped organize the Maine chapter of the Nature Conservancy, an international group that buys and preserves wildlands.

At the end of the year, Maria Carson was recovering slowly from a bout of pneumonia. In January, Rachel came down with the flu and was sick for two weeks. Marjorie and Roger got the flu next. Rachel took care of Roger because Marjorie had to be hospitalized. Two weeks later, Marjorie died of pneumonia and complications related to her diabetes.

Rachel wrote to Paul Brooks about her niece:

> Marjorie and I were very close all her life, and of course I miss her dreadfully. . . . I shall now adopt Roger as my own; he had lost his father before he could remember him, and in our small family I am the logical one to care for him, and I'm sure, the one who is really closest to him.

Rachel was now mother to a five-year-old boy. Her own mother was 88. In May, Rachel would turn 50.

EIGHT

1957–1958

*"But knowing the facts as I did, I could not rest until
I had brought them to public attention."*

In Silver Spring, Rachel kept Roger busy to keep him
from dwelling on his mother's death. They explored the woods,
wearing yellow slickers on rainy days. At night, Rachel let
him stay up late to see the stars or the full moon, then she
read him *The Tale of Peter Rabbit* or other Beatrix Potter
books until he fell asleep. She settled him into a new school
nearby. Frail Mrs. Carson needed extra care too, for she was
still recovering from pneumonia. Overwhelmed with grief and
responsibilities, Rachel found little time to write. She came
down with colds and lost weight. But, typically, she kept her
emotions to herself and seldom complained.

Before Marjorie's death, she had bought an acre of land
in Silver Spring, and construction was underway on a house for
herself and her mother. Now Rachel reviewed the blueprints
with her contractor—she needed a bedroom for a little boy.

Almost every day, Rachel drove to the construction site
to see what progress had been made. She picked out windows,

doors, and doorknobs and decided on paint colors. One thing Rachel was sure about: she did not want any useless bric-a-brac. The house must be simple-looking and functional.

Rachel, Roger, and Maria Carson finally moved in. Rachel vowed to regain her health and to follow a schedule that included writing. In her new book-lined study, she reviewed the text and layout for an illustrated children's edition of *The Sea Around Us*. From her window, she gazed into the woods that surrounded the house. Friends stopped by, enjoying the breeze on the screened-in porch. One of Rachel's cats often darted about the porch.

That same year, Rachel accepted an assignment from *Holiday* magazine. They wanted an article about the "pristine beauty" of the seashore for a special upcoming issue called "Nature's America." Rachel fired a letter off to Marie, saying she would be happy to do the article, but added that "no one could write . . . of such a shore today without also leaving in his readers' minds . . . that very few such places remain."

In "Our Ever-Changing Shore," Rachel wrote poetically of the mist over the marshes, a flock of gulls, wide beaches, of the full moon and the tides, and of the changing shore as a result of human influence. She also noted that roads, fishing shacks, and refreshment stands now dotted the once wild seacoast.

She urged her readers "to convert some of the wild areas that remain into state and national parks." Some areas should stay untouched, she believed, as if people did not exist. "For there remains, in this space-age universe, the possibility that man's way is not always best."

Everyone praised "Our Ever-Changing Shore." One of Rachel's many friends, Curtis Bok — author, sailor, and judge — wrote, "Oh what a *lovely* piece. . . . Wonderful, wonderful. . . .

A clean South Carolina inlet, above, *and marine debris,* left

You take people right to the shore so that they walk there and feel it and understand it."

With Paul Brooks, Rachel discussed the possibility of expanding the article into a small book. Rachel's theme—as in her article—would be her concern that people should save some of the wild places of the earth. Dumping of trash, real estate development, and an increase in the use of manufactured chemicals, such as DDT—scientifically known as dichloro-diphenyl-trichloro-ethane—were changing not only the coast, but the entire country.

Trash left behind on the Atlantic shore

For years, Rachel had worried about pesticide use. Way back in 1945, when she was trying to earn extra money by writing articles, she had written to *Reader's Digest* about doing an article on DDT.

> Practically at my back door here in Maryland, an experiment of more than ordinary interest and importance is going on. . . . The experiments [on the use of DDT] . . . have been planned to show what other effects DDT may have if applied to wide areas: what it will do to insects that are beneficial or even essential; how it may affect waterfowl, or birds that depend on insect food; whether it may upset the whole delicate balance of nature if unwisely used.
>
> I believe there is a timely story in these tests.

Reader's Digest was not interested. Because of her family and job demands at the time, Rachel never asked other magazines about the DDT article. For her own benefit and education, however, she continued to read numerous government reports, including those dealing with the dangers of widespread use of pesticides. Few pointed out potential long-term serious consequences of DDT.

Rachel knew that the manufacturing of DDT and other deadly poisons was on the increase. By the late 1950s, more than 200 new chemicals had been developed to kill insects, weeds, fungi, and rodents. Farmers, homeowners, gardeners, and others spread millions of pounds of pesticides across the United States and around the world.

The corporations that produced pesticides raved about the "magic" of DDT and similar chemicals, saying that they saved farmers time, money, and labor. The corporations poured enormous amounts of money into advertising these products with such newspaper ads as "War on Insects" and "Bad News for Bugs."

Many of the insects that had been sprayed with DDT began to produce offspring that were stronger and immune to the pesticides. Rachel knew that the chemicals climbed the food chain, first by entering plant and then animal life. Eventually the pesticides reached human tissues and organs, causing an increase in illnesses and diseases, such as cancer. She wondered if these new chemicals might trigger genetic changes or cause later generations to have physical and mental abnormalities.

Along with her personal interest in the hazards of pesticides, Rachel was involved in other projects. She was considering writing a book called "Remembrances of Earth," which would be about the continents, when she received a letter that changed her plans.

Olga Owens Huckins, a friend and former newspaper writer, lived in Massachusetts, where she and her husband had a private bird sanctuary. That year, the whole area was sprayed from the air for mosquito control. In January 1958, Olga wrote to the *Boston Herald* and sent a copy of her letter to Rachel.

A dead clapper rail in its native salt marsh

The 'harmless' shower bath killed seven of our lovely songbirds outright. We picked up three dead bodies the next morning right by the door. They were birds that had lived close to us, trusted us, and built their nests in our trees year after year. The next day three were scattered around the bird bath. (I had emptied it and scrubbed it after the spraying but YOU CAN NEVER KILL DDT.) On the following day one robin dropped suddenly from a branch in our woods. We were too heartsick to hunt for other corpses. All of these birds died horribly, and in the same way. Their bills were gaping open, and their splayed claws were drawn up to their breasts in agony.

Air spraying where it is not needed or wanted is inhuman, undemocratic, and probably unconstitutional. For those of us who stand helplessly on the tortured earth, it is intolerable.

Rachel set aside her work to inquire about how to help her friend. In Washington, D.C., she asked the experts for information. The more she learned about pesticides, the more upset she became.

Rachel called her agent, Marie, explaining that very little information about pesticides was appearing in newspapers and magazines, and suggested that Marie find someone to write an article on the subject. In the meantime, Rachel made phone calls, wrote letters, and read reference books. What she learned about the mass application of pesticides horrified her. She reluctantly considered writing the article herself.

Marie checked with *Reader's Digest, Ladies' Home Journal, Woman's Home Companion,* and *Good Housekeeping,* all widely read magazines at that time. All four magazines rejected Rachel's article idea. One editor doubted whether the information for such an article could be substantiated.

During this time, Rachel followed a New York court case involving the use of pesticides. A Long Island group of citizens went to court to protest the aerial spraying of DDT to get rid of the gypsy moth. The spraying went ahead, saturating gardens, farms, ponds, and salt marshes. Commuters, children at play—anyone outside—were drenched by the oily mixture. Birds, fish, crabs, and useful insects died. So did a horse who drank from its contaminated water trough.

Rachel could not attend the trial. She wrote to E.B. White, author of *Charlotte's Web* and *Stuart Little*. His essays in the *New Yorker* criticized humanity's arrogant attitude toward nature. "Take up your pen against this nonsense [the spraying to kill gypsy moths]," she pleaded. "There is an enormous body of fact waiting to support anyone who will speak out to the public."

While the citizens continued to fight the case in court, Rachel corresponded with them and received all 2,000 pages of testimony. E.B. White wrote to Rachel, "I think the whole vast subject of pollution, of which this gypsy moth business is just a small part . . . starts in the kitchen and extends to Jupiter and Mars." He encouraged her to contact William Shawn at the *New Yorker* and write the story herself because he had other commitments.

Although not a crusader, Rachel decided to write about the dangers of pesticides. "The time has come," she said. "There would be no peace for me if I kept silent." She agreed to write a magazine article or work with someone on a book. She stepped up her correspondence with every scientist who knew anything about pesticides. She clipped articles. She checked and double-checked fact after fact. Files of notes and letters from experts around the world covered her desk. One by one, she read them and sent off responses.

A plane sprays pesticides to stop locust infestation.

Before long, Rachel realized that no one else was available or experienced enough to write about pesticides. She agreed to write an article for the *New Yorker*. On May 22, 1958, she also signed a book contract with Houghton Mifflin. The working title was *The Control of Nature*. Rachel thought the book would be ready for publication by January 1959. After that, she had lots of ideas; one was to write a book about exploring nature with children.

NINE

1958–1962

*"I could never again listen happily to a thrush song if
I had not done all I could."*

For the first time, Rachel's research did not include tide pools in Maine or the laboratory at Woods Hole. She dived into a mountain of technical material. Day after day, she read volumes of government testimony. Instead of going to Maine right away, she pored through research books in the libraries. She wrote to every independent scientist in the United States and Europe who knew anything about pesticides.

As summer ended and autumn approached, Rachel spent more and more time with her ailing mother. That September, she helped Roger make the transition from kindergarten to first grade. She hung up his drawings and followed his schoolwork closely. When he was sick and home from school, Rachel nursed him, as well.

In early December 1958, Maria Carson died. It was a severe shock to Rachel since she and her mother had been so close. And now Rachel accepted the sole responsibility for

Roger, who had lost his mother and great-grandmother in the same year. A few weeks after her mother's death, Rachel wrote to a friend about her mother:

> Her love of life and of all living things was her outstanding quality. . . . And while gentle and compassionate, she could fight fiercely against anything she believed wrong, as in our present Crusade! Knowing how she felt about that will help me to return to it soon, and to carry it through to completion.

Rachel returned to her work in February. She sent her editor a progress report. "All the pieces of an extremely complex jigsaw puzzle are at last falling into place. . . . It is now possible to build up, step by step, a really damning case against the use of these chemicals as they are now inflicted upon us."

Work went slowly. Rachel had underestimated the time it took to read all the technical papers and to write letters seeking clarification of point after point. She wrote that she felt "like the Red Queen [in Lewis Carroll's *Through the Looking Glass*] who had to run as fast as she could just to stay where she was."

That year, the New York lawsuit failed. Rachel, who had closely monitored the case, was upset. Evidence introduced in court seemed to prove that DDT was harmful. The lawsuit was thrown out of the United States Supreme Court on a technicality.

After returning from Maine, Rachel hired Jeanne Davis to be her secretary and general assistant and they soon developed a close friendship. Not only did Jeanne have a Ph.D. in economics, but her husband was a doctor and an expert on cancer, so she knew the medical terminology and could research books at the library for Rachel.

With Roger in school, Rachel worked nonstop with an almost religious zeal, often going to bed late and rising early to organize her thoughts before Roger stirred.

She worked closely with Dr. Clarence Cottam, a distinguished biologist and an old friend at Fish and Wildlife. Dr. Cottam spoke out publicly against the misuse of pesticides while Rachel quietly collected evidence for her book.

They wrote to one another frequently and Dr. Cottam replied in one letter, "It seems to me you have gone deeper into this subject than anyone. . . . Because of the controversy I doubt that it will ever be a best seller."

A tractor spreads pesticides on a field of corn.

Lois and Louis Darling's drawing for the title page of Silent Spring

Dr. Cottam was referring to the subject of pesticides. The chemical-manufacturing companies were making millions of dollars with their new products, like DDT and chlordane. And government agencies, such as the USDA—United States Department of Agriculture—were proud of these products and did not want them discredited. Many biologists wrote to Rachel to give her information anonymously, fearing they might lose their jobs and not be able to support their families.

One scientist wrote about how the insecticide dieldrin was spread in Tennessee to kill the Japanese beetle. Thirty pounds per acre (34 kg per hectare) of dieldrin granules covered a park, he told Rachel, including the picnic tables. Parents had to wipe off the tables before setting out their food.

Some officials labeled Rachel a troublemaker and hesitated to give her information. Although Rachel corresponded with hundreds of individuals, she decided not to disclose the full extent of her project to many of them. Rachel knew she had started a battle and, already, sides were being drawn.

Some scientists offered their assistance. They sent their findings to Rachel. Several doctors, including one from the

National Cancer Institute, helped her with the sections dealing with cancer hazards related to pesticides. Other experts shared their findings from years of research for Rachel's chapter on the effects of pesticides on birds and wildlife.

Rachel was especially upset by the destruction of bird life and knew her readers would be, too. She and Paul Brooks considered naming the chapter on birds "Silent Spring." Eventually, they realized the image of a silent spring symbolized the entire book. *Silent Spring* became the title.

Rachel's efforts to finish the book by 1960 slipped away. Poor health interrupted her work. Like other family members, she battled arthritis. In the spring of 1960, she came down with the flu, then a sinus infection and an ulcer. To Paul she wrote, "I should think it might have waited until the book is done!"

In 1960, an election year, Rachel served on the Natural Resources Committee of the Democratic Advisory Council. For the Democratic platform—the principles and policies of a political party—Rachel wrote about pollution control, radioactive contamination of the sea, and chemical poisoning

Part of the drawing for the opening of the "Needless Havoc" chapter in Silent Spring

of the earth. She pleaded for preservation of natural areas and for passage of the wilderness bill.

She returned to *Silent Spring* and, at the same time, took on another big project, the revision of *The Sea Around Us* for Oxford University Press. Her preface to the new edition warned against pollution of the oceans with atomic wastes. In the last paragraph she wrote:

> It is a curious situation that the sea, from which life first arose, should now be threatened by the activities of one form of that life. But the sea, though changed in a sinister way, will continue to exist; the threat is rather to life itself.

Exhausted much of the time, Rachel struggled through each day. Recurring bouts of flu sent her back to her doctor. Later that year, she received bad news. She had cancer.

Gulls land on oil slicks in the once-clean harbor of New Haven, Connecticut.

A breast tumor that she'd had removed the previous spring had been malignant, but at the time her doctor had decided not to tell Rachel. Now the cancer was spreading.

Rachel matter-of-factly wrote to Paul that a medical expert in the field of cancer "has outlined a plan of treatment that makes sense and reflects his fine understanding, and through him I have gone to a man here [in Silver Spring] who has an outstanding reputation in radiation therapy. So, we have started."

Rachel decided to keep her health problems to herself. That Christmas with Roger, they searched for spruce seedlings behind the house. Rachel pointed to one and told Roger the tree was for the squirrels.

> On Christmas Eve the red squirrels come and hang
> little shells and cones and silver threads of lichen on
> it for ornaments, and then the snow falls and covers
> it with shining stars, and in the morning the squirrels
> have a beautiful Christmas tree.

They played the game again and again, finding the best Christmas tree for the bugs, the rabbits, and the other forest residents.

In a letter to a friend describing Christmas that year, Rachel said, "We had a happy day here—who could help having a Merry Christmas with an eight-year-old boy surrounded by space-age toys?"

By January, Rachel came down with an infection that settled in her knees and ankles. Bedridden for three weeks because she could not walk, she hired two nurses, depending on them and Ida, her housekeeper. With her editor, she discussed ways to write her book more easily.

Despite her illnesses, Rachel enjoyed spring from inside her house. In March she wrote, "This morning began (7 a.m.)

Wild geese fly over a Potomac estuary.

with the cries of geese, and I managed to stagger to the window (shouting for Roger to share the excitement) and get it open in time to hear them better and see the dark, shifting column in the gray sky."

Gradually, Rachel returned to writing. She finished a draft of a chapter on poisons. She decided to have *Silent Spring* illustrated by Lois and Louis Darling, who had done the drawings for a number of books, mostly for children.

By the summer of 1961, when Rachel left for Maine, she had been working on *Silent Spring* for three years. She was anxious to finish her book, because if anything, chemical pesticide use was increasing.

As usual, the cottage provided Rachel with a therapy better than any medicine. She did much of her writing at night, staying up late after she found her second wind. Marie came to Southport to confer over *Silent Spring*; so did Paul Brooks.

While Roger attended day camp, Rachel cleaned the house, went shopping, and planned meals, like any busy parent. On other days, the Freemans' grandchildren and Roger raced across the deck, in and out of the house, and through the woods. Or they played with toys. Sometimes, friends stopped by. They sat on the porch and talked about world affairs and local happenings. If Roger said, "Rachel . . .

Rachel in the garden behind her cottage in Maine

I'm bored," Rachel stopped what she was doing. Sometimes, she and Dorothy would walk through the woods with the three children or explore tide pools below the house.

Years later, Dorothy's granddaughter Martha Freeman remembered outings with the two women. They

> directed my senses toward the mosses and mushrooms of the pine woods, the periwinkles and small starfish in tide pools, the seals and ducks in the sea, the waves lapping the beach and the sun setting into the treetops. I learned no scientific terms. . . . I simply learned to see.

When Rachel closed up her cabin at the end of the summer, she knew that her work on the book was winding down. She polished the final draft in the autumn, and by January, most of the manuscript was in the hands of Marie Rodell, Paul Brooks, and William Shawn, the editor at the *New Yorker*.

After reading the manuscript, Mr. Shawn telephoned to congratulate Rachel. In a letter to Dorothy Freeman, Rachel described her feelings.

> Suddenly I knew from his reaction that my message would get across. After Roger was asleep, I took Jeffie [her cat] into the study and played the Beethoven violin concerto—one of my favorites, you know. And suddenly the tension of four years was broken and I let the tears come.

Silent Spring was serialized in the *New Yorker* in June 1962. Three months later, Houghton Mifflin published the entire book. Many scientists believed that the impact of Rachel's book on the world would be greater than any other since Charles Darwin's *The Origin of Species*, published over a century earlier, which outlined the controversial theory of evolution.

The woods behind Rachel's cottage, where Rachel and Dorothy wandered with the children

TEN

1962-1964

*"The pleasures ... of contact with the natural world ...
are available to anyone who will place himself under the
influence of a lonely mountain top—or the sea—or the stillness
of a forest, or who will stop to think about so small a thing
as the mystery of a growing seed."*

Within two weeks, *Silent Spring* reached the *New York Times* best-seller list, and by the end of the month, it soared to first place. Later, the book would be printed in dozens of languages and have a worldwide impact.

Across the country, newspaper headlines read: "Rachel Carson Stirs Conflict" and "Silent Spring Is Now a Noisy Summer." Newspaper editors and columnists offered their opinions. It seemed as if everyone had something to say about *Silent Spring*. Rachel became the center of a national controversy.

Attacks against Rachel had begun even before the book appeared, but she was prepared. She had checked and double-checked every paragraph, every page, and every statement.

One attack came from the Veliscol Company, which manufactured a pesticide called chlordane. To keep the book from being published, they had threatened to sue Houghton Mifflin over Rachel's information on chlordane. Her publishers rechecked Rachel's information and reaffirmed that she was correct. The case was dropped and the book was published.

At the same time, the National Agricultural Chemical Association spent a quarter of a million dollars to produce a booklet to refute the "facts." They quoted from *Silent Spring* —without Rachel's permission.

Time magazine accused Rachel of trying to frighten the public by "using emotion-fanning words" and referring to her "oversimplification and downright errors." Others claimed that Rachel had taken leave of her scientific senses, calling her a priestess of nature, a bird lover, and a communist. In one of the most widely distributed anti-Carson articles, a well-known nutritionist stated that her book should be ignored.

Reactions to Silent Spring *were both extremely positive and extremely negative. This cartoon, published after Rachel's death, could be interpreted either way—as a celebration by the animal*

Because of her failing health, Rachel made few appearances. But in a lecture sponsored by the National Council of Women of the United States, she answered her critics.

> There are those who would have you believe I advocate that we abandon all chemicals tomorrow and turn the world over to the insects. Those who say this have not read *Silent Spring* or, if they have, they do not wish to interpret it correctly. It would not be possible to abandon all chemicals tomorrow even if we wanted to. What we can and must do is begin a determined and purposeful program of . . . replacing chemicals with new and even more efficient methods as rapidly as we can.

Silent Spring gained in popularity because of its merit and because of the reputation of the author. An ardent

world of Rachel's balanced approach to ecology, or as an ironic prediction that her views would allow pests to take over the world.

conservationist, United States Supreme Court Justice William O. Douglas called the book "the most important chronicle of this century for the human race." Others, including many nationally known scientists, praised *Silent Spring* and Rachel's courage in writing the book.

Rachel drew inner strength from these comments and from fan mail—most of it favorable. Letters filled her mailbox day after day. She treasured many. One read: "As I drive home along the Hudson [River] tonight I'll feel more human for having read your lovely, loving words today. I know, too, that your great quiet eloquence will open many eyes and close many bottles." Across the top, Rachel wrote, "This alone makes the long travail worth while."

At first, she tried to answer every letter herself, but they came by the thousands. Later, she wrote 10 different replies to cover certain types of letters. After she read each letter, she assigned it a category so she or her secretary, Jeanne, could reply to each one. To Lois Crisler, a writer friend, she wrote, "Now, when there is an opportunity to do so much, my body falters and I know there is little time left."

People from all over the country wrote to Congress, the Departments of Agriculture and of the Interior, the Public Health Service, and the Food and Drug Administration. They sent letters to their local and county agencies. After reading Rachel's book, they demanded that their government do something. And President John F. Kennedy announced the formation of a pesticides committee in his Office of Science and Technology to investigate the situation. Rachel met with the committee members.

Later, the committee released a report criticizing several government agencies while praising Rachel Carson for alerting the public to the dangers of pesticides. For Rachel, it marked a turning point. Now the government was involved. No one could deny that pesticide problems existed.

In May, government hearings on environmental hazards began. When Rachel testified on June 4, 1963, photographers, reporters, and spectators filled the room. Connecticut's Senator Abe Ribicoff opened the hearings. "Miss Carson, on behalf of the Committee we certainly welcome you here. You are the lady who started all this."

Sitting at the long witness table, Rachel addressed the committee in an even voice: "The problem you have chosen to explore is one that must be solved in our time. I feel strongly that a beginning must be made on it now—in this session of Congress."

Reporters noted that Miss Carson did not look like a person who would take on the multimillion-dollar pesticide industry. They wrote that she was soft-spoken, calm, and poised.

In between government hearings and answering letters, Rachel received numerous awards. For Rachel, the most significant was the Albert Schweitzer Medal of the Animal Welfare Institute, which she accepted on January 7, 1963. She told the audience that Dr. Schweitzer "has told us that we are not being truly civilized if we concern ourselves only with the relation of man to man. What is important is the relation of man to all life. I am very proud, and also very humble, to be a recipient of this award."

A few months later, she was named Conservationist of the Year by the National Wildlife Foundation. The Garden Club of America honored her with their highest conservation award, and she received another conservation award from the Isaak Walton League of America. She joined the Board of Directors of the Defenders of Wildlife.

CBS decided to do an hour-long program on the pros and cons of *Silent Spring*, which had sold more than half a million copies in the United States alone. They filmed part of it at Rachel's home in Maryland. Ten-year-old Roger looked over the camera equipment and met the host, news commentator Eric Severeid.

"CBS Reports" aired April 3, even though two advertisers—one selling food products and the other a household disinfectant—withdrew their sponsorship. Eric Severeid opened the program by announcing that the United States had used 900 million pounds (400 million kilograms) of pesticides in 1963.

In her living room with Roger, Rachel watched herself read from her book and press for reforms and controls. After other panelists accused her of being a nosy biddy, fanatic in her defense of "the balance of nature," Rachel stated calmly that science was feeding the public "tranquilizing pills of half truths [while] breaking the threads that link life to life." Thousands of viewers tuned in to "CBS Reports," and, once again, Rachel was the focus of the nation.

That June, Jeanne Davis drove Rachel, Roger—now 11—and the cats, Moppet and Jeffie, to the cabin. Rachel brought stacks of mail to answer, but for the first time, she had no new manuscript to work on. By then, cancer had spread to her bones, causing her to move with difficulty. Even so, she wanted to cook and try simple household chores, despite arthritis in her hands.

Stanley Freeman carried up bucketfuls of specimens for Rachel to view under her microscope. Sometimes, Rachel and Dorothy picnicked on blankets near the house. Lying under an evergreen canopy of spruces and firs, they listened to the ocean and watched songbirds dart about the trees.

The rocky coast of Maine

Dorothy read to Rachel from *The Wind in the Willows* and her other favorite books. On drizzly, damp days, Stanley and Dorothy drove her to her favorite beaches.

The summer sped by quickly. Just before Rachel was to close up the cabin, her beloved cat Moppet became ill. Rachel took her to an animal hospital, delaying her trip home. A few days later, Moppet died and Rachel wrote to a friend that

Rachel reads with the Freemans.

"she is buried in a beautiful spot near our back door to become part of the Maine she loved."

Rachel returned to Silver Spring so Roger could start school. She walked with a cane, and by mid-October, she relied on a wheelchair. Ignoring her health problems, she flew to California to give a lecture. Afterward, she fulfilled a lifelong dream when she visited California's Muir Woods, accompanied by Sierra Club leader and conservationist David Brower. A National Park Service guide slowly pushed her wheelchair among the big redwood trees. For Rachel, the highlight of an already wonderful day came later when she saw some 200 brown pelicans at nearby Rodeo Lagoon.

December was a busy month. Rachel bought herself new clothes for her trip to New York. Joined by Dorothy and Stanley Freeman, who drove her to New York, Rachel received the Audubon Society Medal, the first one given to a woman. Three days later, she accepted the Cullum Medal from the American Geographical Society. The following day, she

*Muir Woods
in California*

attended the American Academy of Arts and Letters and was elected one of the academy's 50 lifetime members. Only three other members at that time were women. Afterward, with Stanley and Dorothy, Rachel was excited that the citation referred to her as a great writer who had "used her scientific knowledge and moral feeling to deepen our consciousness of living nature and to alert us to the calamitous possibility that our short-sighted technological conquests might destroy the very sources of our being."

At the same time, she met with her doctor for X-rays and tests. To Lois Crisler, she wrote that "things look very good and I feel I have been handed a nice new chunk of borrowed time." Rachel went on to ask how Lois was doing and about her writing. "Let me hear briefly, soon."

In mid-January, Stanley Freeman died suddenly of a heart attack, plunging Rachel into deep sorrow and concern for Dorothy. Rachel's own health was precarious. She cherished each day and month and dreamed of one more summer in Maine. She wrote to Dorothy, that it was a war she would lose in the long run, but she intended to win as many battles as possible. In a letter to Lois, she mentioned that perhaps Paul Brooks and his wife Susie would raise Roger.

Rachel Carson died in Silver Spring, Maryland, on April 14, 1964. She was 56.

At a church service a few days later, the pastor read a letter Rachel had written the previous September to Dorothy Freeman after they had witnessed the monarch butterfly migration in Maine.

> But most of all I shall remember the Monarchs, that unhurried drift of one small winged form after another, each drawn by some invisible force. We talked a little about their life history. Did they return? We thought not; for most, at least, this was the closing journey of their lives.
>
> But it occured to me this afternoon, remembering, that it had been a happy spectacle, that we had felt no sadness when we spoke of the fact that there would be no return. And rightly — for when any living thing has come to the end of its cycle we accept that end as natural. . . .
>
> That is what those brightly fluttering bits of life taught me this morning. I found a deep happiness in it.

Monarch butterflies

The great blue heron feeds in its threatened wetland habitat.

EPILOGUE

*"Conservation is a cause that has no end. There is no point
at which we will say 'our work is finished.'"*

Rachel Carson lived long enough to see the immediate
impact of *Silent Spring*. But what about the long-term impact
of the book and of her place in history?

Knowing she was dying, Rachel discussed the idea of a
committee to help inform the public on the status of pesticides.
Friends established the Rachel Carson Council in Washington,
D.C., in 1965. The council focuses on chemical contamination,
especially the pesticide problem explored in *Silent Spring*,
and on Rachel's efforts to provide an understanding of the
complexity and wonder of the natural world. Shirley Briggs,
Rachel's longtime friend, became the executive director of
the council.

As a result of the public outcry inspired by *Silent Spring*,
the government formed the Environmental Protection Agency,
or EPA, in 1970. One of the jobs of the EPA is to test and

regulate pesticides and other toxic contaminants. Over the years, the government has enforced stricter environmental standards, phasing out most uses of DDT and many other hazardous pesticides.

Despite global interest and concern about pesticides, the chemical industry in the United States is thriving. The annual quantity of pesticides manufactured in the 1990s is over four times that manufactured at the time Rachel Carson published her warnings. It is estimated that approximately 8 billion pounds (3.6 billion kilograms) a year are produced worldwide. Many of the chemicals currently used still pose a danger to our environment. Federal enforcement of pesticide regulations remains lax. DDT, the use of which is restricted in the United States, continues to be manufactured in the United States and shipped overseas.

Before her death, Rachel Carson knew that changes in pesticide use would be slow. She asked that we not depend on pesticides, but take "the other fork in that road" that "offers our last, our only chance to reach a destination that assures the preservation of the earth." That "other road" includes preserving land in its natural state.

In her will, Rachel provided generous bequests to the Sierra Club—an organization that promotes conservation by government legislation as well as sponsoring outdoor activities—and the Nature Conservancy—an organization that buys land for preservation. Rachel left money to the Nature Conservancy for it to manage its coastal and island preserves in Maine that border salt water. Those areas are now called the Rachel Carson Seacoast Preserve System.

In 1969, newspaper journalist Ann Cotrell Free, one of Rachel Carson's most ardent admirers, suggested that the government name a wildlife refuge after Rachel Carson. Within

10 days, Secretary of the Interior Walter Hickel had received about 2,000 letters of support from people all over the country.

Free's idea became reality when Hickel named a national wildlife refuge along the Maine coast in honor of Rachel Carson. At the headquarters in Wells, Maine, where a trail loops through the wetlands, Hickel dedicated the refuge on June 27, 1970. To Rachel's friends, he said that "the Rachel Carson National Wildlife Refuge will stand as a high tribute. . . as a salute from a grateful nation, to one who devoted her life to improving the environment for us all." A plaque was unveiled at a woodland site overlooking the tidal marshes and the ocean.

The salt pond—part of the Rachel Carson Seacoast Preserve System—at low tide

Ten years later, on June 9, 1980, President Jimmy Carter addressed a group of distinguished guests on the South Lawn of the White House. He was awarding the Presidential Medal of Freedom, the highest civilian award given in the United States, to 14 notable Americans including Rachel Carson. President Carter gave the medal to Roger Christie, Rachel's grandnephew, and read the accompanying citation:

> Never silent herself in the face of destructive trends, Rachel Carson fed a spring of awareness across America and beyond. A biologist with a gentle, clear voice, she welcomed her audiences to her love of the sea, while with an equally clear determined voice she warned Americans of the dangers human beings themselves pose for their own environment. Always concerned, always eloquent, she created a tide of environmental consciousness that has not ebbed.

Nearly a year later, on Rachel's birthday, May 27, the United States Postal Service issued a 17¢ stamp honoring her. The ceremony took place in Rachel Carson's hometown of Springdale, Pennsylvania.

Today, her childhood home is on the National Register of Historic Places, and it is open to the public. A dedicated group of volunteers maintain the Rachel Carson Homestead—the original house and an acre of land. Volunteers also conduct nature classes for children.

Chatham College, located in nearby Pittsburgh, is also proud of its famous graduate. In 1989, the college organized the Rachel Carson Institute to promote the ideals and spirit of Rachel Carson. Rachel Carson Day at Chatham College includes an essay contest and environmental activities for high school students.

The state of Pennsylvania passed a bill to commemorate the birth of Rachel Carson. It has designated every May 27

Rachel on the porch of her cottage in Maine

to be "Rachel Carson Day . . . in recognition of Rachel Carson . . . who is generally recognized as the 'mother of the age of ecology.'"

Of all these honors, Rachel would have treasured one in particular. At the time of her death, bald eagles, peregrine falcons, and brown pelicans faced extinction. Their numbers were declining rapidly, because early use of DDT had caused these birds to produce eggs with thin shells and deformed chicks. After the use of DDT was restricted in the United States, scientists began to try to save these species by hand-raising chicks. In 1979, three healthy young peregrine falcons were released to the wilds from the roof of the Department of the Interior building in Washington, D.C. One of the falcons was named Rachel.

List of Conservation Organizations

National Audubon Society
700 Broadway
New York, NY 10003

Chatham College
Rachel Carson Institute
Woodland Road
Pittsburgh, PA 15232

Defenders of Wildlife
1244 19th Street NW
Washington, D.C. 20036

National Park Service
Department of the Interior
P.O. Box 37127
Washington, D.C. 20013

The Nature Conservancy
1815 North Lynn Street
Arlington, VA 22209

Rachel Carson Council, Inc.
8940 Jones Mill Road
Chevy Chase, MD 20815

Rachel Carson
  Homestead Association
613 Marion Avenue
Springdale, PA 15144

Rachel Carson
  National Wildlife Refuge
RR 2, Box 751, Route 9 East
Wells, ME 04090

Sierra Club
730 Polk Street
San Francisco, CA 94109

The Wilderness Society
1400 Eye Street NW
Washington, D.C. 20005

Sources

Chapter One

p.9 Paul Brooks, *The House of Life: Rachel Carson at Work* (Boston: Houghton Mifflin Co., 1972), 16. Reprinted by permission of Houghton Mifflin Co. and Francis Collin, Trustee. Copyright © 1972 by Paul Brooks.

p.15 John Masefield, "Sea Fever." Used by permission of the Society of Authors as the literary representative of the Estate of John Masefield.

p.19 Rachel Carson, "A Battle in the Clouds," *St. Nicholas League*, September 1918. Used by permission of Francis Collin, Trustee.

Chapter Two

p.21 Brooks, *House of Life*, 18.

p.21 Ibid, 17.

p.22 Rachel Carson freshman English composition, from Wendy Wareham, "Rachel Carson's Early Years," *Carnegie Magazine*, November/December 1986, 26. Used by permission of Francis Collin, Trustee.

p.22 "The Arrow," Chatham College, Feb 11, 1927. Used by permission of Francis Collin, Trustee.

p.23 Rachel Carson letter to Mary Frye, from Wareham, "Rachel Carson's Early Years," 27. Used by permission of Francis Collin, Trustee.

p.24 Ibid, 28.

p.26 Alfred, Lord Tennyson, "Locksley Hall."

p.26 Brooks, *House of Life*, 18.

p.27 Rachel Carson letter to Dorothy Thompson, from Wareham, "Rachel Carson's Early Years," 33. Used by permission of Francis Collin, Trustee.

p.27 Ibid.

Chapter Three

p.29 Brooks, *House of Life*, 2.

p.31 Dorothy Thompson Seif, interview with the author.

p.33 Brooks, *House of Life*, 20.

p.33 Ibid.

p.34 Rachel Carson, "Undersea," *Atlantic Monthly*, September 1937. Reprinted by permission of Francis Collin, Trustee. Copyright © 1937 by Rachel L. Carson. Copyright renewed 1965 by Roger Christie.

p.37 Brooks, *House of Life*, 3.

p.37 Ibid, 4.

p.37 Ibid, 5.

Chapter Four

p.39   Rachel Carson, Papers. The Beinecke Rare Book and Manuscript Library, Yale University. Used by permission of Francis Collin, Trustee.

p.39   Rachel Carson, *Under the Sea-Wind* (New York: Simon and Schuster, 1941). Reprinted by permission of Francis Collin, Trustee. Copyright © 1941 by Rachel L.Carson. Copyright © renewed 1969 by Roger A. Christie.

p.40   Philip Sterling, *Sea and Earth: The Life of Rachel Carson* (New York: Thomas Crowell & Co., 1970), 104. Used by permission of Dorothy Sterling.

p.40   Brooks, *House of Life*, 69.

p.41   Sterling, *Sea and Earth*, 104.

p.41   Brooks, *House of Life*, 70.

p.42   "The Gentle Storm Center," *Life Magazine*, 12 October 1962. Reprinted by permission of Francis Collin, Trustee.

p.42   Sterling, *Sea and Earth*, 111.

p.44   Brooks, *House of Life*, 79.

p.44   Ibid, 84-5.

p.45   Ibid, 77.

p.45   Ibid, 10.

Chapter Five

p.47   Brooks, *House of Life*, 128.

p.47   Sterling, *Sea and Earth*, 111.

p.49   Rachel Carson, *Conservation Bulletin*, Department of Fish and Wildlife. Used by permission of Francis Collin, Trustee.

p.50   Frank Graham, Jr., *Since Silent Spring* (Boston: Houghton Mifflin Co., 1970), 10. Used by permission of Francis Collin, Trustee.

p.53   Brooks, *House of Life*, 115.

p.53   Ibid, 119.

p.53   Ibid, 111.

p.54   Ibid, 119.

p.55   Ibid, 125.

Chapter Six

p.57   Brooks, *House of Life*, 324.

p.57   Rachel Carson, Papers. Beinecke Library.

p.58   Brooks, *House of Life*, 132.

p.58   Ibid.

p.60   Ibid, 131.

p.60   Ibid, 126.

p.62   Ibid, 128-9.

p.63   Ibid, 129.

Chapter Seven

p.67   Rachel Carson, *The Sense of Wonder* (New York: Harper & Row, 1965), 42. Reprinted by permission of HarperCollins and Francis Collin, Trustee. Copyright © 1956 by Rachel L. Carson. Copyright © renewed 1984 by Roger A. Christie.

p.68   Brooks, *House of Life*, 160.

p.70   Ibid, 153-4.

p.70   Ibid, 158.

p.74   Rachel Carson, *The Edge of the Sea* (Boston: Houghton Mifflin Co., 1955), v. Reprinted by permission of Houghton Mifflin Co. and Francis Collin, Trustee. Copyright © 1955 by Rachel L. Carson. Copyright © renewed 1983 by Roger Christie.

p.75   Sterling, *Sea and Earth*, 142.

p.76   Carson, *Sense of Wonder*, 8-9.

p.77   Brooks, *House of Life*, 207.

p.77   Ibid, 213.

Chapter Eight

p.79   Brooks, *House of Life*, 228.

p.80   Ibid, 214-5.

p.80   Ibid, 226.

p.80   Rachel Carson, Papers. Beinecke Library.

p.83   Brooks, *House of Life*, 229.

p.85   Ibid, 232.

p.86   Ibid, 236-7.

p.86   Ibid, 237.

p.86   Ibid, 228.

Chapter Nine

p.89   Brooks, *House of Life*, 272.

p.90   Ibid, 242.

p.90   Ibid, 243-4.

p.90   Ibid, 248.

p.91   Ibid, 251.

p.93   Ibid, 263.

p.94   Rachel Carson, *The Sea Around Us* (New York: Oxford University Press, 1961), xiii. Reprinted by permission of Francis Collin, Trustee. Copyright © 1950, 1951, 1961 by Rachel L. Carson. Copyright © renewed 1979 by Roger Christie.

p.95   Brooks, *House of Life*, 265.

p.95   Carson, *Sense of Wonder*, 40.

p.95   Graham, *Since Silent Spring*, 33.

p.95   Brooks, *House of Life*, 266-7.

p.98   First published in *Maine Times*. Used by permission of Martha Freeman.

p.98   Brooks, *House of Life*, 271-2.

Chapter Ten

p.101   Rachel Carson, Papers. Beinecke Library.

p.103   Brooks, *House of Life*, 301.

p.104   U.S. Supreme Court Justice William O. Douglas.

p.104   Brooks, *House of Life*, 299.

p.104   Ibid, 300.

p.104   Rachel Carson, Papers. Beinecke Library.

p.105   U.S. Senate hearings.

p.105   Brooks, *House of Life*, 309.

p.105   Ibid, 316.

p.106   Rachel Carson, Papers. Beinecke Library.

p.108   Ibid.

p.109   American Academy of Arts and Letters.

p.110   Rachel Carson, Papers. Beinecke Library.

p.110   Brooks, *House of Life*, 326-7.

Epilogue

p.113   Rachel Carson, National Audubon Society acceptance speech, December 1963. Used by permission of Francis Collin, Trustee.

p.114   Rachel Carson, *Silent Spring* (Boston: Houghton Mifflin Co., 1962), 244. Reprinted by permission of Houghton Mifflin Co. and Francis Collin, Trustee. Copyright © 1962 by Rachel L. Carson. Copyright © renewed 1990 by Roger A. Christie.

p.115   Walter Hinkel, Department of the Interior Papers.

p.116   President Jimmy Carter, Public Papers of the Presidents of the United States.

Bibliography

Books and Articles by Rachel Carson
(In chronological order)

"A Battle in the Clouds." *St. Nicholas League* (September 1918).

"Undersea." *Atlantic Monthly* (September 1937).

Under the Sea-Wind. New York: Oxford University Press, 1952.

The Sea Around Us. New York: Oxford University Press, 1951.

The Edge of the Sea. Boston: Houghton Mifflin, 1955.

Silent Spring. Boston: Houghton Mifflin, 1962.

The Sense of Wonder. New York: Harper & Row, 1965.

Papers. The Beinecke Rare Book and Manuscript Library, Yale University.

Other Sources

Brooks, Paul. *The House of Life: Rachel Carson at Work.* Boston: Houghton Mifflin, 1972.

"The Gentle Storm Center." *Life Magazine* (12 October 1962).

Graham, Frank Jr. *Since Silent Spring.* Boston: Houghton Mifflin, 1970.

Sterling, Philip. *Sea and Earth: The Life of Rachel Carson.* New York: Thomas Crowell, 1970.

Wareham, Wendy. "Rachel Carson's Early Years." *Carnegie Magazine* (November/December 1986).

Index

Photo Acknowledgments

The illustrations have been reproduced through the courtesy of:
pp. 1, 2, 8, 11 (bottom), 14, 16, 18, 20, 28, 32, 38, 58, 73, The Beinecke Rare Book and Manuscript Library, Yale University; pp. 2-3, 76, Schmuel Thaler; pp. 6-7, 127, Mark A. Klingler; pp. 11 (top), 99, 115, Ginger Wadsworth; pp. 13, 17, used by permission of Rachel Carson Council, Inc.; pp. 24, 25, Archives, Chatham College; p. 35, John Clifton; pp. 36, 70, 112, 118, 128, David Molchos; pp. 43, 51, 60, photographs by Shirley Briggs, used by permission of Rachel Carson Council, Inc.; pp. 46, 71 (top), 107, Tony La Gruth; pp. 48, 81 (top), Jeff Greenberg; p. 52, NOAA National Marine Fisheries Service; p. 55, Center for Environmental Education, Washington, D.C.; pp. 56, 72, U.S. Fish and Wildlife Service/Rex Gary Schmidt; p. 61, Wendy W. Cortesi; pp. 65 (top), 68, 97, 108, 117, Stanley Freeman, Jr.; p. 65 (bottom), Pete Honig; p. 66, Alfred Eisenstaedt, Life Magazine © 1962 Time Warner Inc.; pp. 71 (bottom), 96, Doyen Salsig; pp. 74-75, Bob Hines/The Beinecke Rare Book and Manuscript Library, Yale University; p. 78, The Bettman Archive; pp. 81 (bottom), 82, Center for Marine Conservation; p. 84, Connecticut Coastal Program Staff; p. 87, FAO; pp. 88, 100, © photographs by Erich Hartmann, used by permission of Rachel Carson Council, Inc.; p. 91, Agricultural Extension, University of Minnesota; pp. 92, 93, drawings by Lois and Louis Darling from *Silent Spring* by Rachel Carson. Copyright © 1962 by Rachel L. Carson. Reprinted by permission of Houghton Mifflin Company. All rights reserved. The Beinecke Rare Book and Manuscript Library, Yale University; p. 94, Ingert Gruttner; pp. 102-103, reprinted by permission of UFS, Inc.; p. 109, National Park Service; p. 111, U.S. Fish and Wildlife Service/Milton Friend.